South African-born and raised, Tracy Swinson presently resides in Cape Town. Tracy Swinson is a cultivator of positivity by inspiring people to ignite their resilience and encourage people to be unbreakable. She is a company entrepreneur, author, mother of three and current keynote speaker. Tracy adores poetry, literature, and the arts. She was a candidate in 2007 for the Marie Clare South Africa Business Woman of the Year award.

This book is dedicated to the cherished memory of my mother, Margret Helen Hunkin, who lived from 1947 till 2004, taken too soon by breast cancer. After thinking about my life without my mother's hand in raising me in my early years and teaching me resilience without my realising it, I was inspired to write about overcoming adversity and smiling in the face of death. My mother used to tell me that if you can write a book about your life, you have lived it fully. There is always a beginning and an end. You are the author of your story; make it yours and own it.

Tracy Swinson

UNBREAKABLE

AUSTIN MACAULEY PUBLISHERS™

LONDON ∗ CAMBRIDGE ∗ NEW YORK ∗ SHARJAH

A CIP catalogue record for this title is available from the British Library.

ISBN 9781035832002 (Paperback)
ISBN 9781035832019 (ePub e-book)

www.austinmacauley.co.uk

First Published 2024
Austin Macauley Publishers Ltd®
1 Canada Square
Canary Wharf
London
E14 5AA

Nicole Douglas

Greigan Douglas

Kyle Douglas

Megan Dywer

Tina Da Silva

Estelle Ferreira

Ilidio Carlos Ferreira

Dr C Benn

Dr J Slabbert

Dr G Demetriou

Shawn Hogg

Michelle Van De Langenberg

Barrie Bookstone

Paula Lamb

Andre Kruger

Cynthia Smith

Derek Milne

Jan Van Rensburg

Tracey Louise Douglas

Coleen Denisiuk

Milpark Hospital

Donald Gordon Oncology

Dr F Snyckers

Debra Matias

Daniel Derkson—Writing Studio

Marlon Smith—Photographer and Editorial assistant

Table of Contents

Preface

I wrote this book about my life story because my life is very much like a grape that is plucked from a vine and stomped on. From a perfectly rounded ripe fruit to being squashed, stomped on and having all the life squeezed from its skin. This process, it becomes something different, a beautiful-bodied fine wine.

As a happy little girl, I never imagined that life would throw me so many curveballs and crush me the way it did. I have been shot, overcome two bouts of cancer, domestic violence and despite all this, I found resilience.

I was able to come through the process of being crushed to imparting my story of resilience into a glass for everyone to sip on; the person I am today is far better than that grape that was at first plucked from that vine.

Chapter 1
Down the Rabbit Hole

"Penny for your thoughts, Mum?" I hesitantly asked.

The late afternoon passed over, casting a dark shadow over my mum's face where she stood hushed, staring vacantly out of the window into the garden with its lawn stretching from the lavender hedge with an iceberg rose creeper crawling up a grey wall, with a rolling green lawn to our front door.

I had been observing her for a while in silence, watching her shoulders stoop as she stared. She was tall with black hair, lilac blue eyes, rosy cheeks, and pink lips, always calming me with her gentle smile and soothing voice.

My heart shattered sensing a darkness in her soul when she turned to me, tears glistening in her bright eyes, unprepared for what she was about to tell me.

Taking a deep breath, her soft, gentle voice jarred me when she revealed how she wanted to take her life so desperately, and mine.

I never knew that my mother suffered from depression and that she tried to take her life. Always happy, even in her darkest times when I was growing up, it upset me that only at the age of 33, I got to know this dark secret she withheld from me.

#

Margaret's bird's-eye view of the traffic ten floors below her did nothing to convince her not to jump.

She balanced one foot on the balcony, ready to take the leap, balancing her other foot on the chair. Her yellow chiffon maternity dress swayed in the wind, delicately framing the life that she carried within her. Her beautiful eyes filled with tears, her cheeks were flushed, and her black hair clung to her neck from the summer heat.

The noise of the traffic from below drowned out her thoughts, she was about to jump to her death, taking her unborn baby with her. Feeling unburdened and euphoric, this heaviness was about to end. Death was not something she feared, but life.

Ken walked towards the kitchen of the small Hillbrow flat he rented with Margaret.

Ken was a very arty, charismatic person with a bigger-than-life personality who proudly sported rose tattoos that he got when he signed up to join the Navy. He was not accepted into the Navy due to an injury he had and became involved in martial arts, representing South Africa in 1969 before disappearing from our lives.

He had mixed emotions about my mum's pregnancy and about the marriage. Things hadn't been going well lately between them and he knew that both he and Margaret were unhappy.

When he reached the kitchen door that fateful day, a flutter of Margaret's yellow chiffon maternity dress caught the corner of his eye. He turned towards the balcony and his heart skipped a beat when he saw her on the edge of the balcony.

He ran across the lounge, his heart beating in his throat, and slipped on the rug as he sprinted towards the balcony. Adrenalin catapulted him back on to his feet as soon as he hit the ground, he ran and grabbed Margaret around her waist pulling her off the ledge.

She crumpled in his arms in despair, sobbing softly, "Leave me alone. I don't want to live anymore."

#

Two months later, I was born on my mum's birthday. And so, begins the story of my life, destined to be an interesting one with never a dull moment.

Shortly after I was born, my father left my mother and I and we were forced to move into my grandparent's home which offered a foundation and some stability for the next six years of my life.

My Gran's house was a face brick-house with a red tin roof. There was a bay window in the lounge that looked onto a rose garden. It was my Grans' hobby to grow different roses. My favourite place was a storage cupboard where all the cleaning material were kept and doubled up as a pantry.

I took my crayons and colouring book and closed the door to escape from the madness in the house. I also remember Gran's many trinkets in the lounge on display which fascinated me, and an apple tree in the backyard with a sandbox which I loved to play in.

The backstairs was my special place to sit with my grandfather. The stairs were tiled in slate and was cold sitting on them in winter but a treat in summer it cooled the butt down.

Oblivious to the fact that I had no father in my life those six years, holds some of the most precious memories I carry.

I remember my grandpa Ken, or Pop as I called him, with tenderness. He was a thin, lanky man whose blue eyes sparkled with an omni-present smile on his face.

Pop was my hero; I would follow him around the house like a puppy dog. One of my memories is the fuss I would kick up when he left for work in the morning. It was standard procedure for me to wait at the gate and watch him walk up the road, dreading the moment he would turn the corner and would be lost to me for the day.

I would scream blue murder for him to come back, which he would dutifully do at least three times every morning before I eventually settled down.

Every afternoon I would wait for him at the gate, filled with joy when I saw his lanky long legs come around that corner and head towards me with a huge smile on his face.

I looked forward to every afternoon when Pop sat on the kitchen stairs with his tin of black shoe polish and his one pair of work shoes. I sat next to my Military Hero as he fondly shared stories of his battles during the 2nd World War, how he had been captured by the baddies.

I loved the stories he told me, always in an interesting, by-the-way kind of tone, in order not to frighten me. Describing the big brown army tanks, fighter planes and artillery, I had endless questions: "Why were people fighting?" "Does it hurt when you die?"

Being an only child, I had a fairly vivid imagination. Although he toned down the tales he spun, I could see the people lying on the ground surrounded by smoke, imagining the noise of bombs dropping and fighter planes flying overhead. I was never frightened though; his soothing voice and his matter-of-fact narration left me in awe of what he had seen and done.

Despite the first six years of my life being my happiest childhood memories, as in most households, we had our fair share of skeletons in the cupboard.

Friday nights were pay day, bringing the fruits of the harvest, not only was the kitchen be re-stocked with groceries needed for the following week but so was the fruit of the vine. (or should I say wine?)

This is the one dark blur on my childhood memories of Pops. As much as I loved him, Friday nights would turn him in to someone I didn't recognise. *Someone to fear.*

There would be loud banging and angry voices behind closed doors and in the morning my Gran would emerge from her room with scars and bruising I hadn't seen the night before. I have one recollection of Gran throwing a steel clock at my Pop's head, before being pulled into the bedroom as a small scream escaped from my mouth.

My mum was amazing at distracting me from these moments. They would soon be relegated to the back of my mind until the next episode occurred.

Saturdays were subdued, on Sundays we headed off to church and on Mondays everything returned to normal before the pattern would start again. I remember vividly on one occasion my Pop had left a full glass of beer on the steps where he would polish his shoes. There was no-one around and I was curious as to why his golden liquid was left on the stairs, knowing I should not touch it, but my curiosity got the better of me.

I quickly downed this golden liquid before anyone could see. I head back into the house and when I reached the passage, I could not feel my legs and slid down the side of the wall. My mother came out of the bedroom, realising something was up with me. She picked me up and could smell the alcohol on my breath. She gave me a teaspoon of Panado syrup and put me to bed. I could hear in the next room my mum was speaking quite loudly to my Pop. I was sad because I got my Pop into trouble.

Pop had found a new drinking buddy whenever he had that last sip of beer in his glass, he would call me and give me the glass with the last of the golden liquid in it to finish off. This became our fun little secret…

I will never know what demons he fought. My heart aches for the pain he felt that turned him from a wonderful loving man to an ugly drunk.

Before I turned five years old, my granddad went away and never came back. I knew Pops would not return.

I never fully understood where he had gone, heaven was a vague place for me. Pops deserted me and my heart ached for something I didn't understand, his stories sung a tune to my heart with the smell of shoe polish and the soothing sound of his voice. As the days without him rolled by, I understood that he was not coming back. There was a void in my heart.

Who was going to tell me war stories?

And then we were three.

My Gran and mum were prominent figures in my life. They both worked hard and always had so much love and encouragement to give.

Watching them, I created my favourite game of dress up. I pretended to work with random papers on my Fischer price play telephone, bossing Gran and my mum around.

My mum told me I could be anything I wanted to be. My dreams of what I would be one day would change on a weekly basis I would go from being a fighter pilot to a singer.

In my mind, anything was possible if I believed it.

My Gran was always well-groomed.

I watched her get dressed for work in the mornings, completely fascinated as she put on her brooch, pearl earrings, and necklace that was kept in a silk jewellery box that played a tune when she opened it and a ballerina spun in circles while the music played.

Gran put a little make-up on—back then it was blue eye shadow with a little rouge on the cheeks—then she dabbed some on her lips.

I stood pouting so I too could have some rouge on my lips before leaving for play school. This was the highlight of my day.

Without me evening knowing this, is where my resilience training started.

Having to walk six arduous blocks to nursery school and back through all seasons, my mum was a pro at distracting me with this nursery rhyme: "This is the house that Jack built, this is the malt that lay in the house that Jack built…" By the time we got to 'this is the cow with the crumpled horn' we had already walked two blocks in the direction of the nursery school. There was an urgency when we got to 'this is the farmer sowing his corn' because the school building was in sight, and we had not finished the poem. Without me realising that I walked six blocks without asking my mum to carry me.

Afternoons, I would wait in anticipation for my mum to fetch me after she had finished work.

She had a different tactic for the walk home which always involved a new or favourite pastry. Keeping it as a surprise despite my question "What did you get me today?" she allowed me to nag her a bit.

A few blocks in, Mum revealed the surprise pastry: Mouth-watering cannoli or petit fours. My mother would feed me the pastries in bits in between discussions of *Alice in Wonderland* which was my favourite story while growing up. When I complained about my feet being tired, she quoted the *Cheshire cat*.

"Would you tell me, please, which way I ought to go from here?" Alice asked.

"That depends a good deal on where you want to get to," said the Cheshire Cat.

"I don't much care where—" Alice replied.

"Then it doesn't matter which way you go," said the Cheshire Cat.

"—so long as I get somewhere," Alice added as an explanation.

"Oh, you sure to do that," said the Cheshire Cat, "if you only walk long enough."

Before long, we arrived home. I did not even realise that I had walked a total of 12 blocks in one day.

That was quite a distance for such little feet.

#

It was a day like any other when I waited impatiently at the school gate for my mum to fetch me, anticipating my treat.

The treat for that day was far bigger and better than I could have imagined. Standing beside my mother was a man whom she referred to as my father.

I ran to my mum who swooped me up and said, "Today Daddy is driving us home, so we don't need to walk."

The word *daddy* felt strange. It was not a word that ever crossed my lips. Now, this stranger had this title. I could see my mum was happy and that made me happy.

I have a vague memory of weeks later. It was spring. I remember seeing such beautiful colours on the way home one Friday afternoon.

That weekend, there was a lot of fuss, food being prepared, dashing back and forth.

My Gran kept me occupied in her room with me unpacking her silk jewellery box and putting the jewellery neatly back into it.

Little did I know that this was the day my mother and pastor dad were getting remarried again. I heard voices then silence. Quietly slipping off my Gran's bed, I tiptoed to the door. Slowly looking around the corner, saw my mum in a pretty cream coloured dress. I didn't care much for my dad as I felt like this was a change I was not ready for.

Before long, I was allowed to join in on the wedding celebrations with family members and friends of my parents. They drank a lot of champagne and merrily clinked glasses, standing around talking and laughing, some danced to some music that played in the background.

There were mostly finger snacks. I remember the sausage rolls, which were my favourite. I put some on a plate and took it to the back garden, where I sat under a tree with my Gran and shared it with her.

I wondered what it would be like to be a grown-up and talk about grown-up things instead of all my imaginary adventures and conversations I would have with a dead military man.

I never really understood what we were celebrating. My life was about to change drastically the happiness I knew in my soul was about to change.

A few adjustments needed to be made with regard to our new living arrangements but crawling into Gran's bed instead of mums was a small price to pay to have Dad home.

Things just seemed to be getting better and better. I was excited to hear we would be moving to our own house where I would have my own bedroom and I would get to choose the colour of my room.

#

18

Number ten Carter street was a cul-de-sac with only 6 to 12 houses in the street. At the bottom of the cul-de-sac, a pathway led up to a *valley and hills*.

The three-bedroom house had wooden floors and large windows done out very 70s interior as it was that era. There was a fig tree in the back garden that my Siamese cat Chang and I would climb. I would eat figs while Chang sat next to me. My bathroom had a semi round bath with a step up to get into it I was really fascinated by this bathroom. The kitchen was a fair size and nicely lit as it was north facing it was the gathering place for conversation while my mum cooked meals.

One week after moving into our new home, my mother and father had a horrendous argument. I remember my mother crying all night while my father slept on the couch. This was unsettling to me as it reminded me of my Pop and Gran fighting. The next morning, my mum walked me to school and told me she will pick me up again when school is out. I could see the hurt in her eyes and that she had been crying. I asked her if she was okay, and she told me everything was going to be alright.

When she fetched me after school, we walked in a completely different direction to where new home was. We stopped outside an apartment block.

I asked my mum why we were here, she knelt down and told me in a very gentle voice, "This is going to be our home for a while."

I was so confused, but the idea of having my mum to myself was not a bad prospect. A month later, almost to the day, my mum arrived at my school with my dad and we travelled back into the direction of 10 Carter Street. They had made amends and I was back to sharing my mum again.

Number 10 Carter street would become our new beginning as a family.

For a long time, I wished for a family like my friends had and it soon became clear that you need to be careful what you wish for.

My previous fun loving carefree *you can be whatever you want to be* slowly started to disappear from my life.

Dreaming and imagining were snuffed out and stifled very quickly, when in my excitement of moving my record collection which I danced to, could not be found. Dancing to Pop music was not regarded 'Christian-like' by my pastor dad. It was also not Christian-like to dance, go to birthday parties, have friends come play or even have a sleepover.

I pined for the days of dancing to Elvis, The Beatles, and many other records in my collection but what I missed the most, was the ability to express myself and dream.

Living the new dream, living with my dad and in our new house, and being walking distance from my primary school, was a treat.

When I turned seven years old, I was allowed to walk to and from school.

#

I walked routinely to and from school with my friend, Belinda, a pretty-plump blonde girl with long curly hair, blue eyes and dimples.

One afternoon on a summer's day, when it was so hot that we could feel the tar through our school shoes as we tottered home lazily, we saw a white car that was parked on the corner just before the last stretch home.

A man opened the car door and asked me for directions. I stepped closer, looking warily at the paunchy bald old man with dark eyes. Before I knew what was happening, he grabbed hold of me. To my horror, I saw that his genitals were exposed and screamed. Belinda dropped her school bag and grabbed hold of me, pulling with all her might. The old man lost his grip and let go of me, quickly shutting the car door and speeding off.

When I arrived home hot and flushed from the heat, adrenalin pumping through my veins, I called my mum and told her what had just happened. She rushed home and whisked me off to the police station with my friend, Belinda.

A few days later, I found myself walking through a line-up to identify the old man that tried to abduct me. Both Belinda and I were terrified as we stared through the glass, looking into each man's face, identifying the old man who almost pulled me into his car.

Belinda and I talked to a police officer, telling him the events of that day.

My mum did not give me many details about what happened to the old man, only that he was locked up and 'wouldn't be able to bother little girls anymore'.

#

Spare the rod, spoil the child was an adage that was held firmly when I was a child. I often had the welts and red marks to prove it.

20

There were so many unspoken rules it was hard to keep up what was acceptable and what wasn't.

As a young girl, it was difficult to understand an unforgiving thrashing, and then be told to get on your knees and ask God forgiveness. None of this made any sense to me. I kept being told in Sunday school that God is kind and gracious but why would he want me to be punished like that?

The hidings from my dad became so severe that I could not hold my bladder in fear of him.

I became rebellious. Began lying to escape that prison called home, spending time with my friends, trying my best to fit in without becoming an outcast at school because I was not allowed to leave the house.

I found myself being excluded from most events at school as I was known as *the girl who was not allowed out.*

I spent a lot of time on my own. No longer having fun conversations and laughing with my mum. She seemed always in a mood never wanting to do much, and there was this constant look of worry on her face. This was strange for me as I had never seen this side to my mother.

I would say I was going to stay with my Gran but would be with my friends going to house parties and drinking.

The one Friday night I had asked my parents if I could sleep over at my Gran's house, and they agreed. My Gran was quite easy-going with me because she could see I had no life while living at home so when I stayed over, she allowed me to go out with my best friend, Pam.

One night, we got dressed to go to our favourite club in Hillbrow Bella Napoli. We never had enough money for a taxi, so we decided to hitch-hike to Hillbrow after putting our thumbs up. A car stopped, I got into the front seat and Pam climbed in behind the driver.

The man asked us where we were going, we told him and he said he was only going as far as the town. We told him that it was fine and we will walk the rest of the way. As we chattered, he turned off the main road and drove in the direction of a secluded area called Wemmerpan. We asked him what he thought he was doing, and he did not answer.

When he pulled up and turned the car off, locking the doors from his side, I immediately started to panic, Pam asked him to open the doors and let us out.

"Not until I've had some fun," he replied.

At this point, I was looking for something to break the window with. In a split second, Pam pulled a switchblade from her bag and held it at his neck, where I could see a little trickle of blood where the blade sat. She told him to let us go.

I was in complete shock. Pam had always been a quiet happy-go-lucky person. I never realised she had such a dark side.

The man quickly unlocked the doors of the car.

We were fearless, recklessly hitching another lift to the club.

One other Friday night, I went to my gran again, telling her that my friend Pam had been invited to a house party. We got a lift with other friends and went to their party. Being the youngest girls at the party did not bother us. We danced and had fun until we heard a police car arriving. Everyone scattered in different directions.

Pam grabbed my arm. We left out the back door. She jumped up onto the wall and told me to follow as she landed on the other side, then started to run. I was not far behind her.

Everything morphed into slow motion when I spotted a big black dog attacking her, grabbing her by her denims, playing tug of war, ripping her pants, as she made a beeline for the gate. It was a close call but we both got out of there with little to no damage other than a rip in her denims. When I recall the events of that evening, I always have a good giggle to myself. It looked like a scene from a movie scene, her running in slow motion and a dog wrestling with her denims.

Thank goodness my dad never found out! I would have paid dearly for lying and doing things that were not Christian-like, beaten black and blue would have been my punishment.

#

I often wished I had a sibling to share this burden of being a pastor's daughter. However, many years of practice I became skilled at taking on the role of the pastor's daughter during church services. I would smile and be polite but deep down, I was screaming inside my soul, just wanting to break free from all the limitations and restrictions.

For instance, having to sneak out to attend my dance classes and dance competitions placed me under huge amounts of anxiety. I was always on the edge waiting to be caught out and having to face the rod as always and then repent for my sins.

By the age of sixteen, things became volatile between my dad and me, I had been pushed to my limit. I arrived home one afternoon from school, only to find that my bedroom had been turned upside down, my closets emptied out.

My diary where I wrote all my deepest heartfelt conversations with myself, was now exposed as my father had read my diary as well as the oral contraceptive that my mum had arranged for me to be on as I started developing acne. My last shred of privacy other than a door had been completely stripped away. I was not sure how much more I could take.

When my dad confronted me, I told him that my mother had arranged for me to be on oral contraception. He did not believe me and told me to wait in the bathroom until my mother got home from work. When she arrived home, she confirmed that she played a part in arranging my oral contraception for my skin. This was the one time I did not get a thrashing but it caused a huge blowout between my mother and father.

I was not dating anyone at this point or should I say I wasn't allowed to but I did develop a close bond with a boy whose parents went to my dad's church and we were in the same school together, he was three years ahead of me. We hung out quite a lot and I developed a crush on him.

He decided to ask my parents if he could take me to movies one Friday night and my dad said yes to my amazement. After a lovely evening of going to the movies, he drove me home and when he pulled up, he turned the car off. I was chatting away.

When I turned to see why he was not responding to my conversation, he leant in to kiss me. I got such a fright, I had never kissed a boy and was worried my dad would see me, so I head-butted him and broke his nose needless to say he never took me out again until many years later we are still friends today but at a distance.

One Sunday morning, I reluctantly went to church as we would every Sunday. Later during Sunday lunch my dad asked me to do something, and I told him after I was finished eating I would do it.

Talking to him in such a flippant way, the conversation went from zero to a hundred when my dad tried to grab me to give me a hiding.

I completely lost my temper and punched him in the face. When my mum tried to separate us, I pushed her so hard, she fell over.

An explosion of emotions that were bottled up over the last ten years surfaced: Growing up in a religious strict home with such rigid rules like no music, no friends being able to visit, no boyfriends and only going to church services weekends and weekdays, all I wanted was to have a normal life like my friends and have cool parents.

Growing up as a young girl, being the pastor's daughter was extremely difficult not because I had to follow the faith and set a good example.

I got front row seats to things a young child should never be exposed to and seeing demons being cast out of people in the congregation terrified me. Sitting there watching bodies twisting and turning on the floor while foam oozed out of their mouths, screaming and hissing, this left me having nightmares. I would lie in bed while my Siamese cat Chang would comfort me for hours before I was able to go back to sleep.

Often, while on the bus to school, I would look around at people and wonder how would I even know if anyone on the bus was possessed by demons. Not everyone believes this is a thing, but I can confirm for many years as a young child, I witnessed supernatural things happen in front of me.

My mum told me later it looked like two alley cats fighting in the passage that afternoon. I could tell it broke her heart seeing us coming to blows like that.

My mum was, for as long as I can remember, the buffer between my dad and myself. She lived on tenterhooks trying to keep the peace between me and my dad.

I often wonder what would have happened if she just left me to have my say and not get involved. Would things have been different?

After our afternoon tussle, Dad gave me an ultimatum. If I wanted to live in his house, I had to follow his rules or leave.

I left without looking back.

#

I was tired of the severe hidings and the unwarranted discipline, moving back to my Gran's house, which became my home for about eight months before I moved into my own apartment in Hillbrow at the tender age of seventeen.

It was a small price to pay to have my freedom and myself. Not walking on eggshells the whole time.

If you can dream, you can do anything!
By Tracy Swinson

Chapter 2
My Daily Bread

I remember going to view places to rent in Hillbrow that I could afford, which was not much.

Renting a bachelor apartment that had a lovely view of Parktown where I could see the lilac Jacaranda trees in the distance, just below me, the racket of passing cars and sirens felt as if I was living on the road itself.

I saved enough money and was able to buy the necessities such as bed, fridge, and linen.

I felt like I was finally independent. Free.

I felt invincible. Unstoppable.

It was my choice, mine alone which was liberating after living under my dad's thumb.

The ability to buy the necessities gave me a sense of responsibility. I was ready to embrace my freedom. I could put my own personal stamp on everything.

My place was very minimal compared to living in a fully furnished home. It was sparse but it was my own space. I was able to be anything I wanted to be and could do anything if I put my heart into it.

It took me a while to figure out who I was and form my own identity.

I morphed quickly when times were hard.

I lost that innocent look and dressing style; I was more edgy in the way I dressed. My whole wardrobe took on a new life. My space on my walls was covered with the art I liked. My space took on my personality after a couple of months.

When I signed the lease that afternoon, I watched the landlady open a huge cabinet on the wall where she then took the keys for my flat and handed them to me with a welcoming smile.

I was fascinated by the evil-eye pendant she wore around her neck. A short-fat Greek lady with salt and pepper colour hair and a lovely olive skin, she had a happy-go-lucky attitude. She always wore an apron over her clothes as she was always baking.

The next day, I moved into my new home.

I spent the day cleaning and moving the little furniture I had around this big empty room until it felt right. Surprisingly, there was rather a lot to unpack when I looked over at the boxes stacked against the wall. My body was already aching from moving the heavy bed and fridge around and hauling the boxes up the stairs.

This was it, I thought to myself as I sat alone in my flat in the middle of Hillbrow, quietly listening to the noises and taking in my new surroundings.

I felt completely alone in this big world, excited, yet apprehensive of what was to come.

Looking at how sparsely my apartment was furnished; it was clear that it was going to take me at least two more jobs to buy furniture to fill this empty space and blank walls.

The moon light from the night sky lit up the room as I didn't have enough curtains to blank out the peering light.

My footsteps echoed as I walked to the bathroom to run myself a lovely hot bath and to soak away the ache from my muscles.

Soaking my weary body in a lovely hot bath, I forgot that I was all alone. My head reeled with thoughts of how I was going to cope.

Gun shots and sirens shook me from my daze as I shot upright in the bathtub with bubbles clinging to my skin, as if hearing it themselves.

Reality set in.

You have to toughen up fast to survive this life, I whispered to myself. Gun shots and sirens was something that I was not accustomed to.

I barely slept that night, tossing and turning, listening to all the traffic and strange noises rousing my fear.

It sounded a lot like what you would see in a ghetto scene from a movie: scoundrels brawling, music blaring in the background, raucous screaming, overbearing conversations, and traffic passing.

I was up early the next morning, still feeling tired from the move and not getting enough sleep, I had an interview and wanted to be prompt, really needing the job to pay the rent.

Dressing in a suit, I put on my make-up, tying my hair back.

Before leaving, I glanced at myself in the mirror resting up against the wall as I had no tools to secure it on the wall, to make sure that I looked professional for the interview.

Getting this job meant the world to me. I would be independent, pay for my food and rent.

Being a grown-up is not that hard, I thought.

Little did I know what awaited me.

#

I sat in the reception area, anxiously waiting to meet the manager for my interview.

Two other candidates waited to be interviewed. They looked a lot older than me which meant they definitely came with more experience.

I sat in a trance. Chanting in my head, this job is mine, this job is mine.

Was I wasting my time going through this interview? What were my chances really?

When my name was called, I was ushered into an office off a garage that was filled with rental cars.

The garage was underground and was dimly lit. It smelt damp and was cold. There was very little sunlight. Pipes that ran from one side to the other. You could hear the water splashing as it ran over head. One pipe was green and slimy from leaking for some time.

Papers were strewn all over the desk in the office. A sad-looking cup of coffee sat lost amongst heaps of paper, coffee stains left its mark on the paper where the cup had been picked up and put down numerous times.

The manager stomped into the office and plopped down into her chair that squeaked as she pulled herself closer to the messy desk. Jinx introduced herself, she was short with brown long curly hair and brown eyes.

"Why do you want to work for us?" she asked. She was always direct and to the point.

"I just moved out of home into my own apartment and need to pay the rent," was my honest reply.

Jinx looked at me for a moment, then asked, "When you can start?"

I could not believe that I had the job, never even giving thought to the two other candidates who waited to be interviewed.

Two days later, I was working for a car rental company for minimal wage.

I was so grateful for this opportunity and accepted it willingly. This was a great start, things were already looking up and I loved that I was learning something new. I made friends with the other girls working there, but a really good connection with Paula whom is still a close friend to me today.

I quickly became the top rental agent. Recommendation letters streamed in on a regular basis from clients. Instinctively, I knew the value of good customer service to get repeat business, keeping clients from going elsewhere.

Jinx rarely smiled, she was very militant with the staff when she spoke. She kept her private life very private. Very rarely did she join the crew after work for drinks but when she did, she was so different to the boss at work she was wild and fun, hard to imagine they were the same person.

As the months flew by, I realised that this was not going to be enough to pay bills and for me to study further.

I took a part-time job waitressing at a friend's coffee shop in Hillbrow.

This very quaint coffee shop held a continental feel to it. The interior of the shop was outdated. Although it needed a revamp, it was always packed. Its famous coffee and cake selection and the friendly atmosphere kept patrons coming back. It definitely had a certain charm to it.

Late afternoons were always busiest, with Greek men playing Backgammon, laughing, and having heated conversations.

I just loved it there, but the pay was still not enough. Some months I barely made it to the end of the month and would live on boiled eggs, cheese and Provita snacks, longing for a homemade meal or a lovely Sunday roast at Gran's house, but that was now a thing of the past.

I tried not to dwell on it as it made me ache for my gran and my mum.

Happy memories flooded my mind: Home cooked meals, conversations when getting home, that Sunday lunch, the comfort of knowing made me ache for what I could no longer have it was not an option. Talking about my day or just having a cup of tea and watching them cook dinner. Going for long walk with my mum. That familiar smell of home—every home has a distinct smell.

Fond memories of my gran I have today even in her Alzheimer's, such wonderful conversations of her memories and life experiences that always brought a smile to my face. The memory I love most is when she asked me if I could keep a secret.

I replied, "Yes."

She shuffled up to me and whispered "I was naughty when I was younger, your real grandfather is Harry Oppenheimer."

I will never know if she had a crush or if it was true but her eyes twinkled when she told me about her Harry and it was often as she would have no recollection of our conversation.

My new home at first just smelt like fresh paint.

I thought about my gran, how relieved she was when Pops died. It was an end to the cycle of abuse she took on a weekly basis. She never spoke much about him after he passed.

My mum really loved my dad. To her destruction, he was so bad for her.

Over the years, I watched him break her down emotionally and mentally. She never said anything bad about him, but I do recall one evening we sat down for dinner.

He took two mouthfuls of food and then said to my mother that her cooking was terrible and that he wouldn't even feed it to the dog and got up and went to the bedroom.

My mum was a brilliant cook. One night, when he wanted something else for dinner, he decided to engineer an argument. She followed him to the room.

I stood outside the bedroom door and saw that the cupboard door was open.

My dad cursed at my mum. For the first time, I saw her retaliate. She kicked him so hard, he landed in the cupboard. She then proceeded to lock him in the cupboard and told him when he changed his attitude, she would let him out.

It wasn't funny at the time, but I do giggle about it today. After that, he just treated her so badly, proving what a narcissist, the Man of God truly was.

When I clocked off from work one afternoon, I decided to take a stroll from work to home through Hillbrow.

Deep in thought as I walked along the uneven paving, it took me back to my childhood walking from home to nursery school.

Overcome with feelings of nostalgia, I was not really noticing all the people pushed passed me. In my head, I started to recite the house that Jack built poem I fondly remembered from all the walks to and from nursery school with my mum. It brought a smile to my face. The walk home in high heels did not seem so bad after all.

In the distance, I heard someone call my name. I looked up, seeing Lexi, who was my best friend that went to school with me.

We lost contact with each other after I left school to join hairdressing college. It was too far to travel to the south of Johannesburg to go to school, so I enrolled in college to do hairdressing. I always cut and dyed friends' hair so I decided it would be a great career but dropped out due to lack of funds.

Lexi ran up to me and flung her arms around me, giving me the longest hug that went on for minutes. I soaked it all in. This was a familiar memory and the fragrance she wore was also a good memory.

"What on earth are you doing here?" I asked Lexi. "You have never lived in the area."

"I'm going to an audition," she said.

I frowned at her.

"For backup dancers," she replied. "You should come with me. The pay is good. Depending on how many shows you book a week."

This was exactly what I needed to not only resolve my financial dilemma, it was also an opportunity to use all those years of dancing lessons that I did on the sly only my mum knew about, to make some money to pay the many bills.

The prospect of not having to stress about money was a pleasant one and to do something I loved so much.

As we walked to the audition, we spoke about all the events that had happened since we last saw each other.

Lexi had just got out of a bad relationship, she was intrigued about my move to Hillbrow, and how the lack of money inspired me to tackle a few jobs.

We laughed a lot about our days at school and bunking together and some other funny things we encounter. Lexi was the bad girl at school and would always rub people up the wrong way. When the girls wanted to brawl, I was the go-between.

We arrived at a seedy-looking building.

Lexi assured me it was safe as we took a lift to the 5th floor. The lift rattled and jerked. We looked at each other and giggled.

Stepping out of the lift we stood at a door, hesitating for a moment before knocking on it. I nervously looked around for an escape route in case anything went wrong.

Lexi wasn't bothered, she always had her head in the clouds, never contemplating thoughts of danger. I loved her for that.

When Hein, a buff, handsome man with long blonde hair, opened the door and invited us in, I was unsure of what the setup was.

Were we going to be sold on the black market? Possibly raped or chopped into pieces? I thought.

Although my nerves settled slightly when we entered the dance studio, I still had the uneasy fight-or-flee feeling.

There were quite a few girls auditioning so we had to wait patiently, having received a dance sequence to study.

I felt a little rusty watching the other girls, who were really good. Fortunately, I did Tap and Modern dancing with Lexi, my best friend.

After each group finished their routine, they were told that they would receive a call-back if they were successful.

My stomach was in knots, we were up next with a group of older women.

The count down and music started. Before I knew it, it was over.

Nine of us were asked to stay and repeat the dance. We lined up and flew through the dance moves.

The choreographer added onto the dance sequence. We were given five minutes to prepare, then lined up and went through the dance routine. By this time, my feet were killing me.

My mind reeled.

If it's meant for me to be part of the dance team, I will be joining them.

"If I call your name, please stay," Hein announced.

Both me and Lexi were called out with some other girls.

We were elated until Hein said, "Please remove your tops and bras."

I looked at Lexi and whispered, "Did I hear right?"

She nodded and whispered, "How bad do you need the money?"

I hesitated for a moment.

Although I was conflicted, I decided to accept the challenge and removed my top and bra, standing with Lexi and the other girls like soldiers ready for inspection.

Hein stealthily walked up to each of us, taking a good look at our breasts without touching us.

"Right girls, let's do the routine without your tops on!" Hein instructed.

Is he just a pervert or the real deal? I questioned myself.

After we finished the routine topless, Hein told us, "Put your shirts back on and take a seat."

That little voice from my childhood said: *God is still watching you.*

I chose to ignore this as we sat down and as he paraded up and down.

"You will be female dancers at exclusive Gentlemen's Clubs throughout the country. You will be called the Cover Girls. No clothing is required except a G-string and nipple caps," he informed us.

I looked at Lexi, who frowned at me, then boldly asked Hein how much we would be paid.

"For each routine, we will be paying $ 80 plus tips."

Back in the 80s, that was a lot of money.

We signed a two-year contract and began our routine training for our first opening night.

Only years later did I find out that Lexi was having an affair with Hein and that is why she was so confident we were going to get in.

A lot of marketing went to our first night, for which we had two sessions booked.

All I could think about was that I did not have a clue how to be a sexy seductress. It concerned me that my first performance might mark the end of my contract. I had no problem with the dance routine, I just needed to spice it up. A lot.

Being the tomboy amongst my friends, being sexy was going to be a tough challenge.

I was a bundle of nerves not knowing what to expect, thinking of all my body issues. I was not sure how I was going to go through with this. I was overwhelmed, but excited at the same time.

When we arrived, we got our make-up and hair done. Our costumes were beautifully made and looked classy—as classy as you can get with your breasts out and butt exposed.

Back stage was old and musty. You could smell the cigars and alcohol mixed in the air with Cuban music paying in the background and voices getting louder.

I peeped through the old velvet heavy curtains. I could feel my nerves kicking in when I saw how packed the club was.

When I returned to the girls, I couldn't contain my excitement.

"This place is packed girls!" I said.

Lexi ordered some Tequila shots to calm our nerves.

If Dad knew what you are doing, he would kill you, I thought, also thinking, *How are you going to pay your bills this month?*

That trumped my thoughts on what my dad and mum might think, or anyone else for that matter.

I knocked back a second Tequila and focused my thoughts on what lay ahead.

The DJ popped his head in, telling us that the show would be starting in five minutes.

We rushed on stage and took our places. I took a deep breath as the curtains opened at the sound of the music.

As the spotlights illuminated us, we stepped into our group routine, bringing the rousing crowd to their feet after our performance.

Surprisingly, the men were well-behaved at this opening evening, they never once tried to grab or pull on any of us which was a huge relief but if you saw the size of the bouncers, I don't think they had a chance.

This encouraged us to swiftly continue our group and solo performances. The first set went off without a hitch. We were all relieved and excited.

I took in all in the smells, the music, the wooden dance floor, the sound of laughter and Cuban cigars. You are probably wondering how I knew they were Cuban cigars. Well, my mum kept her crochet needles in Cuban Cigar containers and every time she opened them, I would get this smell that I never forgot.

Not in a million years did I imagine this is what I would be doing with my life.

Our dancing required that we should interact with the crowd, titillating men seductively, touching them playfully, leaving them hot under the collar, begging for more.

The bigger the tease, the larger the tip!

I was so nervous during my solo dance that when I removed my top it caught on the nipple caps and as I pulled my top off I could feel the nipple caps peel back of onto the top.

In my mind, I was laughing, thinking this could only happen to me—the preacher's daughter. I wanted the stage to open up and swallow me up.

I carried on like normal, as if it was part of my routine. Being seductive during my erotic dance routine, I realised how easy it was to have men eating out my hands.

I slowly traced my fingers up my legs, and then over my breasts, maintaining full control and eye contact, gently biting my bottom lip as I slid off my chair into a split, rolling on to my back, arching my back as my hands ran up the sides of my body until the music faded.

I was relieved when my solo was over, sitting devastated backstage, convinced that I had thrown my name away.

When we were dressed, we were allowed to go and order drinks at the bar.

The clients waited eagerly, happy to pay for our drinks.

A few men shoved what I thought was paper in the back of my jeans pocket only to find out when I got home that night I had made a lot more than the $200. This must have been the effect of the wardrobe malfunction, my nipple caps coming off.

Fortunately, I managed to learn the tricks of the trade, and continued to seduce clients to the best of my abilities, having many of them attend more than one of my performances at the clubs we danced at.

That night was a sensation. Bookings streamed in fast and furious. Some nights we would do four sessions back-to-back at two clubs.

Some days at work, I would be exhausted from only a couple of hours sleep but it was a means to an end for me.

I regretted nothing. If I had to, I would do it all again.

It taught me a lot about myself. I learnt to love my body.

When growing up, showing too much flesh was a taboo. Sinful.

I had a lot of issues around my body and never thought it was good enough or looked right.

I soon got over that.

You do what you need to do to bring the bread home.

#

As months passed by, me and Lexi would hang out at parties and clubs, enjoying our freedom.

At one of the house parties, my friend introduced me to her neighbour. He was an advocate, a strange-looking short man, who was balding slightly, and had a big nose and stubby fingers.

During the night he kept on begging me to dance with him. All I wanted was to sit and chat.

When he pulled me again, I stood up, towering over him and in a firm voice, said "SIT!"

Before I knew what was happening, he was on all fours sitting like a dog.

I thought this was hilarious and decided to talk to him like a dog: "Sit, stay, walk, roll over…"

He dutifully obeyed, following all instructions.

This attracted an audience. People circled us as I put my foot up on the chair.

"Lick my toes," I said.

He did. Obediently.

Everyone roared with laughter. They thought he behaved that way because he was drunk, but he was sober.

When I was ready to leave, he gave me a piece of paper which I shoved into my handbag, thinking it was his number.

Creep, I thought to myself.

When I rummaged through my bag the following day, I pulled the piece of paper out, to my amazement discovering a cheque for $50 with his number on the back.

I thought this was rather strange, but I decided to bank it.

The advocate called me about two weeks later asking if I would come see him at his office as he had a proposition for me.

When he ushered me into a huge corner office, I sat quietly.

Awkwardly, with beads of sweat running down his bald head that he brushed away with the back of his hand, he asked me if I would be interested in seeing him once a week and to do what I did to him at the party.

My mouth was going dry. I found his offer very peculiar.

"I'm not a prostitute," I stammered.

He laughed, explaining that it was not sexual.

"I just want you to dominate me," he said. "Do we have a deal?"

How could I refuse? I shook on it, agreeing on $50 a session. No clue what that even meant, I had to go off and try do some research. Thank goodness for the Hillbrow underground market, one could find all weird and wonderful things there. It was not long until I had found enough reading material to understand what a dominatrix was.

#

Arriving at his dimly lit office in Braamfontein that first night, I wore a studded leather dress that was so tight it looked like a second skin, showing off all my curves, with a studded collar around my neck.

My make-up was really dark around the eyes, accentuating my shocking red lipstick.

He was wearing a badly fitted suit and a very busy tie and could not help but notice an orange round clock on the wall that was resting on a really bad choice of wallpaper.

After exchanging a few words, I requested payment up front. I winged it in case things went badly. At least, I would have got paid for my time.

He handed me cash this time, which I put it in my bag, placing it on the chair.

I immediately barked orders at him to sit, remove his shirt and tie and the rest of what he was wearing except his socks. He dropped to his knees and in a flash, his clothes lay on a heap on the floor. I tied a homemade doggie-tail band around his waist that hung covering his butthole.

I took out a dog collar and put it around his neck and stroked his head.

"Good boy," I said, taking two bowls out of my bag. I put water in the one and dog food in the other.

I commanded him to lie down and to roll over, then to bark which he did without hesitation.

I could not believe I was doing this. It was insane. I was totally amused, intrigued with my newfound superpower to make a grown man behave like a dog.

I sat in his chair, resting my feet on his desk, watching an esteemed advocate perform whatever I asked him to do. I was praying that he was house broken because I was not going to be cleaning any mess.

As an encore, I removed my shoes, commanding him to lick my feet clean which he did rather eagerly, as any obedient dog would.

I realised at this point that I was good at this and actually enjoyed the power it gave me.

He pleasured himself while I packed up my things and snuck out, leaving him in his delirious doggy state of mind.

#

Before long, I gathered a few more exclusive clients but it was no longer as *tame* as the doggy stint. These were all referrals from my advocate doggy.

As a seasoned dominatrix, I delved deeper into the darker side of the human psyche exploring pain-for-pleasure, fetishes like latex, coloured wigs, and extremely questionable sleazy venues.

NDA's, Waivers and Safe words were the new lingo.

I was earning enough money to rent a small apartment that was sparsely furnished, rigged with all the right equipment to accommodate my clients, from shackles to whips, blind folds, gag balls, masks, paddles, blades, and different types of cuffs…

Nothing could stop me. I enjoyed what I did. For my clients, it was therapeutic.

Psychologically, it was ultimately about relinquishing power for a short time, living out a fantasy to the extreme.

There was one client in particular, a high-powered business mogul with a dark soul. He had no time to spare for his family, but would indulge in our sessions, no matter how much time he wasted.

Another regular client, David, arrived after a hectic day at the office, and was anxiously anticipating the session.

I was dressed in a red latex body suit with a mask and black lipstick.

He took immense pleasure out of pain and requested to be shackled, requesting me to stand on him with my stilettos until they broke his skin, and insert two thick pins through his foreskin.

After he undressed, I shoved him onto the bed and tied him down hands and ankles tightly secured and then blind-folded him so he could not see what was about to come.

I lit candles to start with, playing music in the background.

As I walked over to him, I could see little droplets of sweat on his forehead. Straddling him, I proceeded to slowly drop hot wax onto his chest, his nipples, down his stomach and over his genitals. All the while spewing insults at him, telling him what a useless waste of space he was…

I could see his skin turning red around the hardened wax.

He was now breathing heavily with excitement. I could see in some places little blisters forming and yet he never used the safe word.

I stood on him with my heels until I could see the skin break and traces of blood…then moved onto the piercing of the foreskin.

How broken one must be to enjoy this kind of pain, I thought.

When the session was over, he peeled off the wax. He beamed. He had definitely enjoyed the session and booked his next one right then.

There's very little that can make my stomach turn but for the first time I felt ill.

It wasn't long before I had eight regular customers on my books, high-powered businessmen wanting me to dominate them, it wasn't sexual. For them, this was about relinquishing power and becoming subservient.

I always kept it very professional, never got caught up in why I did all of it for money.

Until the following session satisfied this need, my clients would get dressed and resume their regular lives hiding a very dark secret inside.

#

Life was good, I was 18 years old, earning a fortune and living in a stunning apartment with expensive furniture.

I had a boyfriend who was extremely jealous and possessive. If someone in a store dared to look at me, he became passive-aggressive.

When he found out what I was doing to make money, it sent him in a downward spiral. He was not pleased with me dancing erotically at Gentlemen's Clubs. He asked me to choose between him and my dancing. I told him I will consider it if he would foot the bills I could not pay.

It was a toxic relationship. He was possessively jealous and sometimes abused me physically when our fights turned physical and nasty.

Our relationship see-sawed back and forth. I found myself constantly going back although I knew that it did me more harm than good.

It eventually ended when he got violent and broke down the door to my apartment door to get to me. I had to move without telling him, but he found me, giving me an ultimatum: our relationship or my dancing. I chose dancing.

Needless to say, that our relationship ended fast, which was a good thing. I was elated when it ended, feeling a sense of relief that I did not have to walk on eggshells when he was around.

Little did I know that it was one of many abusive relationships that was to come, that every hardship that lay ahead was born on the back of what of a 17-year-old living alone, struggling to make ends meet and I did.

I was a girl on a mission of survival and independence, not having to stress about paying bills or worrying where my next meal came from.

Realising that no matter how awful a situation might be, I would always fight to overcome any shortfalls, grounding my vigour and resilience, my ability to rise above tricky situations.

I realised that no-one was coming to save me. I had to save myself and learnt very quickly to hustle and take opportunity's when they presented themselves.

I learnt that 'cannot' could not form part of my vocabulary if I was going to overcome hardships in life.

#

One night, my friends wanted to go clubbing. I was not feeling in the mood for it, but after some convincing, I decided to go.

Lexi and I spent two hours getting ready putting on and pulling off outfits until finding something that made us feel fabulous.

We went to a club in Johannesburg across from the Carlton Hotel.

Arriving fashionably late, we were greeted by the familiar faces of bouncers at the entrance.

The music was pumping, the club was filled with smoke.

We went straight to the dance floor and started to dance and laugh.

The DJ, a tall, good-looking man with dark hair and blue eyes, announced that a free bottle of champagne to the best dancer.

How could Lexi and I refuse? We immediately hopped onto a platform and danced up a storm.

When the song ended, the DJ announced that I won the dance-off. I dashed off to claim the bottle of champagne from the DJ, who invited me to have a drink with him when he took a break.

I took the bottle to my friends, shaking it up, spraying champagne all over them. We all had a small sip and before long the bottle was empty.

At this point, this was all Lexi and I drank since we arrived at the club.

I went off to the ladies to freshen up, applying more gloss, teasing my hair a little more. *It was the eighties remember...*

I stood still for a moment, staring at myself in the mirror.

Is this my life? It does not feel real, I thought.

Surely there is more to life than clubbing, erotic dancing, being a dominatrix?

When I left the ladies room, the DJ was waiting for me.

He asked if I was keen to have a drink with him. I agreed and we went to the upstairs bar, where he ordered drinks and we chatted about his job.

It wasn't long before my speech started slurring, my vision blurred. I remember standing up, clinging to the DJ as he escorted me through the kitchen, out the backdoor to a fire escape landing where I started vomiting.

Everything blacked out after that.

An excruciating pain revived me.

I looked around fearfully when realising that I was spread out on a barrel in the pantry. Shouting for help, a hand muffled my screams. Tears streamed down my face as I blacked out again.

I felt a hand on my shoulder, shaking me awake, looking at Lexi, who helped me to the car, where I slipped in and out of consciousness as we drove home.

I awoke the next morning feeling like a train smash.

Stumbling out of the bedroom, I was shocked to find myself bleeding when I inspected myself, raw and bruised, I could not clean myself.

'*Was I raped?*' I asked myself, or was it just my imagination, feeling dirty and shameful, I had three baths that afternoon.

On closer inspection, I noticed bite marks on my back and on the inside of my thighs.

After the doctor examined me, he confirmed my worst nightmare, telling me that I was raped badly and that I should report it immediately.

Although I agreed that I would report my rape, I went straight back home where I slipped into a deep depression. I no longer felt independent or invincible, all I wanted was my mum.

I told no-one about it. I kept my dirty little secret, only discovering that the smarmy DJ was a sexual predator. I was not his only victim, many other girls claimed to have been raped by him.

Why, as a victim of rape, you have to carry the guilt?

I would not allow myself to become a victim. I picked myself up off the floor where I hid from the outside world. Bills needed to be paid.

The young beguiling and innocent girl died that dreadful night.

I developed an intense dislike towards men. As time flew by, I realised that I had never come to terms with my rape.

When we learn to become resilient and do what it takes to live the life we are dealt, only then can you truly live.

Tracy Swinson

Chapter 3
Black and Blue

Shortly after my rape, I ended my dancing and dominatrix careers, believing I had met the man of my dreams.

I left Imperial Car Rental as delivering cars became more and more risky.

When I delivered a car to Sandton Hotel, the VIP client didn't want to come down and sign for his car. As he was a card holder, I decided to just go get his signature. When I knocked on his door, he told me to come in when I walked in, he was not wearing any clothes. I turned to walk out when he grabbed me by the arm. I screamed and he got a fright. I told him he had five minutes to come down and sign or I would take the car back. Which he did.

The last straw for me was when I was delivering to the ANC (African National Congress) building. I was going up in the lift when a group of men crowded around me, tried to assault me sexually, ripping my skirt open and tearing my shirt trying to remove my clothes. I ran down the fire escape, got into our driver's car and went back to the office, immediately handing in my resignation.

I applied for a temp job at Investec Bank, soon joining the permanent staff in the PR department.

Going out with Lexi was still our favourite past time to blow off some steam.

Lexi and I were at Gold Reef City one night, partying up a storm at a pub, having drinks, dancing to loud 80s and 90s music. Dolled up with big hair and oversized shoulder pads, which had been the fashion trend back then, we stood at the bar ordering a drink when two guys came over, offering to buy us drinks. Lexi and I accepted and danced the night away with our newfound friends. Before long, the night was over, and we were invited to have coffee with them.

It was during the early hours of the morning, almost everything was closed except a Bimbo's in Northcliff.

After chatting for a while, I lost interest in the conversation, I was not sure if I was just tired or bored. Halfway through the coffee, I was ready to leave. My gut told me to lose them.

Lexi had made arrangements to meet at a pub a week later to continue our chat and have a few drinks. I was always in the mood for a fun time.

When I arrived, Lexi had two other men with her, Damien, and Brett, who'd spend the other night chatting and drinking with us were a little surprised that Lexi was with someone else so I took it on me to keep Damien and Brett entertained that evening.

Tall and blonde, with blue eyes, Brett was very good-looking, well-built, with short hair and a side path, big dimples, and nice teeth. His buddy Damien was also handsome, he had green eyes and a very naughty look about him, his brown wavy hair was styled in the *George Michael* fashion. Taller than Brett, he was not as well-built, but had an infectious laugh and danced really well.

I was surprised when Brett pitched up at my work and asked me out. Although it was obvious that he had eyes for Lexi, she had met someone else.

From the start, I told Brett that I just wanted to be friends.

During the next couple of months, we became good friends, we did what new friends usually do, go to movies, hang out for lunch.

One night in particular, we went to a house party. Brett and I were having so much fun. Drinks were flowing and music was playing. I remembered during the evening, a guy was so drunk he thought he was outside and unzipped his pants and proceeded to urinate on the hosts indoor plant. We all roared with laughter but I felt for the poor person who had to clean up the next day. While all this commotion was going on, I was dancing with Brett when he leant in and kissed me.

That was that. Our friendship blossomed into a relationship. It felt good, trusting someone in my guarded space. Everything was new and exciting. We fitted into each other's lives and decided to move in together to not only save costs, but to be together.

I discovered that Brett was divorced. He had a son, Adam, of two and a half years old when I met him and was the cutest kid I had ever met. We bonded fast. I liked children but never wanted any of my own. My childhood was not a happy one and I was worried I would never be able to be a good mother.

I found it strange that Brett wasn't home when it was his weekend to spend time with his son, but I never questioned it.

Adam and I did fun stuff together. He was a Ninja Turtles fan, so I always gifted him toys and clothes that was appropriate to the Turtles theme. He nagged me to watch the Turtles on TV, which I did not have, so Brett borrowed one from a friend so that Adam could watch his Turtles during his weekend visits.

As the months flew by, I saw less and less of Adam until I never saw him again.

Brett informed me that he had lost custody.

Being young, I'd never question this. It was all new to me. I did not want to get caught up in the middle of something I had no understanding of. I felt there was more to the story than what Brett told me, but kept quiet, missing my little Turtle buddy.

20 years after my divorce from Brett, Adam reconnected with me and he was telling about a memory he had of his dad marching into their home one Saturday afternoon, causing a commotion, shouting at his mum, then left the house with their television. It shocked me to discover that there had not been a 'mystery friend' whom he borrowed a television from.

At a Football Club fundraiser, which had a back-to-school themed party, I invited Paula, my friend and co-worker at Imperial Car Rental, to join me and Brett. We were thrilled to dress up as schoolgirls, tying our hair back and wearing school uniforms, raring to party up a storm.

Drinks flowed and the music pumped. We danced like there was no tomorrow. When a man accidentally bumped into me on the dancefloor, the smile on Brett's face changed drastically, like I'd never seen before.

I froze fearfully. Before I knew what was happening, a massive fight broke out between Brett and this man, escalating to a rumble in the parking lot.

I felt sick to my stomach watching this violent outburst, blaming it all on them drinking too much alcohol. There was blood everywhere. Brett had lost complete control as he relentlessly punched the man to the ground, kicking him in the head. It took five of Brett's pals to tear him away from the man, forcing him into a car and speeding off.

I dropped Paula off, she was so concerned for my safety I assured her it would be fine she told me she never wanted anything to do with Brett again, she was traumatised by what she had witnessed. I went back to our apartment, anticipating the worst, finding Brett still wrapped up in his fury, pacing up and down the hallway like a wild animal.

I was scared and horrified after witnessing the violent onslaught of his brutal attack.

I woke up feeling ill one morning.

When I was still under the weather three days later, I visited my doctor. Waiting anxiously in the waiting room, it bothered me that I was sick, I planned to travel to Canada and then to the USA.

During my examination I was bombarded with many questions from my doctor, who suggested that I should take a pregnancy test as I was showing all the symptoms. I took the test and tested positive but would not believe it. This was one test I was hoping to fail.

In utter denial, I visited Dr Pretorius, an obstetrician-gynaecologist, who did a sonar and confirmed that I was four months pregnant.

How could this happen? I took careful precaution.

Dr Pretorius was still talking when I interrupted him, telling him to book a C-section as I was not ready to push anything out of my body. He tried to talk me out of it, but I insisted. He calculated the dates and scheduled an appointment for my C-section.

My head was spinning.

How am I going to do this? Be a mother? Tell Brett he is going to be a father for the second time?

I was so nervous I must have practiced that sentence a hundred times: "Brett I'm pregnant."

It all seemed surreal. This was not something I was ready for, and the prospect of termination was illegal.

I cooked Brett a lovely dinner that evening, waiting for the opportune moment to tell him. When I did, he just looked at me. A long silence followed. Then, to my surprise, he asked when the due date was.

I had no idea what was going through his mind. All I knew for certain was that I was prepared to do it on my own.

My life continued as usual. I went to the gym, met up with friends and went out. Not once did it occur to me that I needed to prepare for the baby.

My tummy was showing nicely at eight-months, and I went for regular check-ups.

One morning, my boss, Cindy, called me into her office, she was a short, pretty Portuguese woman with a warm nurturing smile.

"What do you need for the baby?" she asked.

I laughed. "I'm not sure."

She realised I had not bought anything and was still in denial.

The next week, she held a stork party for me at work. Working at a private bank on the banking floor in the PR department, I had made lots of friends. I was surprised and delighted and felt blessed I did not have to buy a single thing.

I was not ready to be a mother. I could not even think about taking on that kind of responsibility.

It was not in my five-year plan or in my plans ever to have children because of my difficult childhood.

Was I destined to be another statistic?

Brett had been married and divorced with a son from his previous marriage. I never really asked what ended their marriage, I had to believe what he told me, that they grew apart. His ex-wife called me once to warn me against him, told me that he had a violent nature. In retrospect, I should have listened to her, but thought she was bitter because of the divorce. Still, her words and voice were etched in my mind.

When the day for my C-section finally arrived, I had packed clothes for the baby and myself, but was unsure what to expect.

After checking into the hospital and being prepped for surgery, Dr Pretorius told me to count backwards. When I awoke, I knew that my life was going to be changed forever. I guess this is what 'grounded for life' means when you have children.

When the nurse came to check on me, she held a tiny bundle of in her arms.

"Here's your beautiful son," she said with a gentle smile.

My hands shook as I carefully took him from her, not knowing what to expect when I cradled him in my arms. I was unfamiliar with the squeaky sound that escaped his tiny body, but when I looked at my son, Kyle, I felt blessed that I was going to be responsible for his life, knowing at that very moment what unconditional love meant, and that I would definitely guard him with my life.

Brett strutted around like a proud dad. We went on with life.

Kyle became my life and everything else secondary. I changed diapers, bathed Kyle, and fed him which never seemed to be enough. He would scream a lot until I found out he had bad colic.

Before long, Brett and I had an argument. I was doing everything on my own with no help, and with a colic baby, I was getting no sleep.

This was the first time, he pushed me up against the wall out of anger. I never thought about that incident again until two years later when he smacked Kyle so hard he fell forward and bruised his nose.

Little did I know this was a warning sign of what was to come.

I am not sure what it is, but all my relationships have been abusive ones.

Was it something I was familiar with because of my granddad? Stemming from my childhood?

#

When Brett and I got married two years after Kyle was born, I guess I was happy, having grown accustomed to how he ruled our lives.

I clearly remember my wedding day.

I sat in the hotel room after many months of planning the wedding to be held in the Little Chapel at Gold Reef City, paying for most of it, anticipating the eagerly awaited day. Sipping a glass of champagne in the hotel room, tears ran down my face. I was not as excited as I hoped to be. It felt like I was making a big mistake.

What are you doing, Tracy? I thought to myself.

I never wanted to get married. I felt like this was not my plan I had for my life. I really wanted to travel the world and just live.

Then Kyle was born.

I felt marriage was such a huge commitment and should only be made when you are absolutely sure this is the person you want to spend the rest of your life with.

Who at 24 knows for sure if this is the person you want to be with the rest of your life?

It terrified me. I felt like it was a trap.

At my age now, it makes sense to commit. You have lived and have a companion to grow old with.

When the horse carriage trotted towards the Little Chapel, I burst out in tears, weeping uncontrollably. The carriage driver had to take me round the Chapel three times. Every time we stopped for me to get out, I started to cry.

My dad waited patiently for me outside the Chapel, waiting to walk me down the aisle. He told me that it was not too late to call it off. I am pretty sure that if anyone else had said that to me I would have fled, but because it was my dad, I was going to show him that I could do this.

I got hold of my senses.

Everyone was already seated when the horse carriage arrived. The Chapel was a small quaint pitch roof with wooden benches and wooden floors, covered in my favourite white roses.

Brett wore his family kilt as did Kyle. They both looked very handsome.

I walked down the aisle and made my vows to Brett and him to me. There was nothing special about our vows, they were the run of the mill vows.

The minister ran through the ceremony without a hitch. Kyle was the ring bearer and when he got up to give us the ring he dropped it, chasing after it as it ran down the aisle towards the church door. It nearly rolled out the door. Was this a sign?

We had such an awesome reception before we went up to the Honeymoon Suite, I felt exhausted and had mixed emotions about everything.

Then Brett came into the room and told me that he was going out, having some drinks with his mates. I was too exhausted to argue and crawled into bed after a long bath, rolling up into a tiny ball.

Is this what marriage was?

Marriage is sacred and I took my vows very seriously.

Marriage is a commitment between two people to be each other's best friends, have each other's back and to always be by each other's side. To stay true to each other. I am a loyal person and I expect the same from my partner and when that dissipates, I can't trust them, and it takes a downward spiral.

For both my Gran and mum, they were both loyal to the bitter end. They took on the role of a wife and mother and fulfilled their duties. I don't believe either of them were every truly happy, but they stayed loyal to the man they married.

I believe you should chose a partner that will go to war with you and I am yet to meet such a person.

#

On my birthday, when I was eight months pregnant with our daughter, Brett had made arrangements to go out for dinner with myself and Kyle.

Kyle and I got ready and waited for Brett to get home.

Six o'clock arrived...then seven then...then eight...Brett eventually arrived at 10 pm.

Kyle had fallen asleep on the couch. When he saw his father he asked, "Daddy, where were you? We have been waiting all night long."

Brett furiously grabbed Kyle and gave him a beating. Heavily pregnant, I had to intervene to protect my son and stepped between them.

"Go to your room and lock the door," I said to Kyle. "Wait for me."

Brett's fury escalated. He turned on me and hit me with a flat hand through my face. It was so hard that I could feel my eye swelling.

Did young boys at school receive tuition on how to give a woman a flat hand and a black eye at the same time?

Grabbing a belt from the cupboard, as he lunged for me, I swung it at him, hitting him on the leg. I am not sure what I was thinking when I did it. He became more enraged, filled with the same anger he had that night when he beat that man to a pulp in the parking garage, grabbing hold of the belt so hard, pulling me to the ground, then began to kick and punch me. I curled up in a ball to protect my unborn child.

This incident happened on the Friday night.

51

On Monday, I was in hospital giving birth to my daughter, branding a black, swollen eye, broken ribs, and a body covered in bruises.

When Dr Pretorius asked me what happened, I lied to him, telling him that I *fell down a flight of stairs.*

He was no fool, knowing exactly what happened, "If you need any help. Just ask me," he said.

I was so badly beaten that I could not hold my daughter Nicole by myself. I spent five days in hospital recovering from an assault instead of celebrating the life of my beautiful daughter. On the day I was discharged from hospital, Brett played golf and I had to ask a friend had to fetch me and my daughter Nicole from the hospital. I remember that drive home I was in tremendous pain my ribs were sore and my body ached but seeing my beautiful daughter made me forget quickly about that beating.

How the hell did this happen? How did I allow it to escalate to this point and lose control?

As the years rolled by, I did not realise that I was a victim of mental and emotional abuse. Fearful and on edge all the time, I never knew when Brett would lose control.

I kept my kids busy and out of harm's way. Brett was never present at any of their birthdays, except for a brief visit when Nicole turned two.

I was a mum working full-time, broken down to a point where I mechanically went through the actions day by day, trying my best to hold everything together.

Brett's loyalty to me and his family was questionable.

I was in denial. Too afraid to be truthful.

Our friends enjoyed our company as a couple. When they visited us for a party at our house, we represented a picture-perfect family but when the doors closed after they left, it was a totally different scenario.

I loved Brett with all my heart but withdrew and hid away from the monster he was.

There was immense tension between me and Brett. We would argue and fight, then make up. He would leave, I would constantly take him back. Making up and breaking up was something we just did.

Realising that Brett had a hard childhood, I would continually make excuses for his behaviour.

It was the typical cycle of abuse.

It was the only thing that made sense at the time. Little did I realise that I lost my self-confidence and esteem and became a total pushover.

Lost my voice.

When Brett accepted a job offer in Durban, I was pleased, thinking that it was the perfect opportunity for us to reconsider how we felt about each other, to see if we could save our marriage.

After a few months, I enjoyed the freedom of being by myself, being alone with my kids, thinking that being a single mum was not such a bad idea.

I was enjoying life, gained some weight, and then a little more, discovering that I had endometriosis, a condition in which cells similar to the lining of the uterus, or endometrium, grow outside the uterus. I was on hormone medication, so picking up weight was natural.

A friend of mine who was pregnant at the time suggested that I should get a second opinion from her gynaecologist and booked an appointment for me.

Taking down my medical history and medication I had been taking, the doctor examined me, proceeding with a sonar scan.

I looked at the screen, not sure what to expect, as my medication prevented my body from producing eggs.

A baby appeared on the screen. I looked at the doctor and laughed.

"That must be the scan from the person before me."

He shook his head.

"It's yours."

I looked at him in disbelief, and I could feel the blood drained from my face. All I could think of was '*No! No!*'

I had felt no movement from this baby I was carrying. Four months later, when I got into my car to drive home, the baby started to kick like mad.

In complete shock, I went to visit my mother the following day.

I needed to see her.

My parents were unaware of my abusive relationship with Brett, the physical abuse I endured. I kept it to myself. The only one who knew about the in's and out's with Brett was a close friend of mine, who had passed away.

I told Mum that I was pregnant, not sure how I was going to cope with three kids.

In her quiet wisdom, Mum knew that I was battling something much larger than another child.

#

I called Brett, insisting to relocate to Durban as soon as possible, ready to start a new chapter in my life.

This is exactly what our marriage needs, I thought.

We found a house both of us fell in love with. Soon, we were living in our new home, waiting for the arrival of our new baby.

The kids were very excited to be moving to the ocean, they could not wait. They were both very happy that they were going to have a baby brother. They loved to lie with their heads on my tummy to see if they could hear him inside me.

Nicole thought this was going to be like having a real live doll.

Kyle was the protective brother and still is today. Nicole was 'daddy's little girl' and could do nothing wrong in Brett's eyes. Today, it is a much different story.

I went for a job interview as a sales executive in logistics, never telling them I was pregnant.

A month later, I told my boss and good friend Colleen that I was pregnant. Colleen was the branch manager and ran the office with ease with an open-door policy where we could talk to her about anything and at any time.

A British citizen living in South Africa, she was a tall, thin blonde woman with a pretty face, and had a brilliant sense of humour. We got a long so well that she had asked me to be her daughter's godmother.

I worked really hard during the pregnancy and things seemed to be going smoothly between Brett and me.

I became a 'golf widow', a woman whose husband spent more time on the golf course than at home. Brett was good at this, doing his own thing.

It was a difficult pregnancy, having backaches and cramps, so before the due date, I went in to see my obstetrician-gynaecologist, who put me on a monitor.

When she returned, I could see that something was wrong.

The next thing I remember was being wheeled into the theatre for an epidural.

Laying quietly and tearful on the operating table, I wondered if my baby was going to be fine. Minutes later, my son Greigan was born. My uterus had raptured when they operated, cutting into my son's forehead, giving him four stitches. Greigan screamed so loud.

I'm sure he woke the dead.

I was in agonising pain the following morning and could not understand why I hurt so much. The doctor informed me that I was torn quite badly, and a lot of internal stitching was done.

Three days later, I was at home with my new baby boy. In pain, I tried not to move around. To make matters worse, Greigan wasn't feeding, screaming for hours.

While showering to get ready for my doctor's appointment, I noticed lines running up my stomach, which looked strange. The doctor told me I had Septicaemia, which occurs when chemicals are released in the bloodstream to fight an infection, triggering inflammation throughout the body.

He put Greigan on formula, as he was starving from not being fed. The doctor also informed me that due to the damage to my uterus, I should consider a hysterectomy, which I agreed to and had it taken care of that same afternoon. I was barely 30 years old at the time.

\#

As the months passed, the fighting started between Brett and I, and the violence flared up again.

I never really understood what caused all this anger but became accustomed to it. I had become an expert at covering up my bruises.

I got a job with RDS. They were looking for a business development person and approached me to apply for the position where I was interviewed by Megan, the branch manager and was offered the job. A thin woman with dark hair and blue eyes, Megan was a chain smoker due to the job being so pressurised.

Megan and I were on our way to a client and Bret called me and my whole demeanour changed. She sensed a fear came over me. When we got back to the office, she called me in and closed the door, asking me if I was in an abusive relationship.

At first, I didn't want to speak to her about it.

"If you need to talk I am here," she said.

A week later, Brett had been physically abusive with me, and she could see the bruises. She encouraged me to get out of my relationship.

It was then that I opened up to Megan and told her about my life at home.

We developed a friendship like no other. We were as thick as thieves. At one point, we even finished each other's sentences and knew what the other one was thinking without saying it.

People often said we had an unspoken language between each other.

Megan was married with a son and daughter who became best friends with my kids. Today, we are all still in each other's lives.

I told her what my life was like. About the abusive marriage I was caught up in.

One image that haunted me was when I was stranded on the highway with a flat wheel when I was eight-months pregnant. I saw Brett drive past me, smiling as he waved at me. To this day, I cannot comprehend how my husband could do that, not stop to help his wife.

It was all part of the abuse.

The situation between Brett and I escalated fast. I felt miserable, not wanting my kids to grow up in a house where the parents were constantly fighting, awaking memories of my childhood when I witnessed the arguments between Grans and Pops.

When Brett got home one evening and a fight ensued, he threw me across the bedroom and slammed the door shut behind him. Before I could escape to the bathroom and lock myself in, he shoved me on the bed and pinned me down. I tried to not make a noise, hearing Kyle standing outside the bedroom door, begging Brett not to hurt me. "Daddy please don't hurt Mummy!" I heard from behind the door.

It was at that moment that everything inside me died. In that moment decided to leave Brett.

During the last year of our unfortunate union, I developed a severe eating disorder due to the constant insults Brett made about my body, forcing me to hate myself.

Now, when I look at photos of myself from back then, I can see that there was nothing wrong with my body.

I had to get away from him without knowing and set a plan in motion.

Megan offered a place of refuge at her home. During the next couple of days, I slowly moved the kids' clothing and a few of my items to her house.

On the evening I decided to leave Brett, I dropped off the kids at Megan's house, then started dinner as if nothing was wrong.

Brett sat working at his computer. When he asked where the kids were, I told him that they were playing at a friend's house.

I had a tight knot in my stomach.

How was I going to do this without getting beaten?

When dinner was ready, I called Brett. My mouth was dry, and I clasped the car keys in my hand.

We sat quietly at the table. I looked up at him and told him that I was leaving.

As I got up and walked to the front door, he stormed at me, shoved me against the wall, trying to grab the car keys from me. I pushed back real hard and dashed to the car. I had opened the gate before breaking the news to him, so my getaway was not that difficult.

My heart pounded in my chest. *I was actually free.*

A smile formed on my face when I turned the corner, then laughed out loud when I thought about the last supper I cooked for him. I wish I could have seen his face when he realised that his favourite lamb curry dish was actually dog food I cooked with curry.

I will never know whether he ate it or not, but the thought of him eating it was good enough for me.

#

The emotional aftermath was a lot worse than I thought when I sat in front of my lawyer, telling him about my marriage, wanting a divorce.

A small balding man with a gentle demeanour, Kobus, stood up from his chair and guided me to the other side of the room where he asked me to look into a mirror and tell him what I saw.

I stared at the stranger in the mirror for a long time, did not recognise the woman looking back at me.

Who is she? I thought. *Where did Tracy disappear to?*

Within seconds, I had a complete meltdown.

Kobus said he would represent me. He wanted me to go for counselling to become mentally agile. He told me that a lot of abused women only managed to go halfway through the process, before they succumbed to the cycle of abuse.

When I started seeing a counsellor, it was difficult at first to talk about my life. As the sessions escalated, it became easier for me to unload my mind. I purged all the horrible experiences: Brett pinning me up against the gate with his car…him choking me until I was unconscious…being beaten black and blue…

The thing that was the hardest to get out of my head was *how I allowed it to happen*, not see the warning signs.

In spite of all our hardship, I still loved him, the man I first met and fell in love with, not the monster he became.

I had to figure out how to let go of Brett, all the bad memories, make the right choice that will be beneficial to me and my children. I found the therapy sessions helpful. It helped me to work through so much heartache.

During the divorce, and even after it was over, Brett and I was still connected, although he had moved on and I brought an end to the booty calls.

How could I grow as a person if I didn't let go?

I lived at Megan's house in the spare room with Greigan, my son shared another room with Megan's son and Nicole with Rebecca Megan's daughter.

I was so grateful that Megan and her husband Rob opened their home to us.

We spent a lot of time with Rob, Megan, and her kids at the beach, or swimming at the house and having barbeques.

The kids used to like to go exploring in the Kloof Gorge and we would spend hours there having a picnic.

Then, the reality sunk in.

I had nowhere to go.

I was almost 31 and had to start over, not having a bank account or a car that was in my name. I started looking for a job that would pay more even though I was working as a waitress in the evenings to make up the shortfall while the divorce was going through.

Although I was exhausted, I focused on having three things: I needed a place of my own, a car, and a new job.

Life was great.

Megan and I were as close as ever and so were the children, we spent many fun times together. Girls just want to have fun.

I had been dead for a long time, lost the lust for life, but as time went on, I felt the spark of life coming alive deep inside of me again. I had total freedom of expressing myself, knowing that good things awaited on the horizon. I could not get enough of my new freedom, although it came with the responsibility of being a single mum raising three kids.

Brett had the kids on weekends.

As a free person suddenly having all the freedom in the world, resulted in a purge of partying until the early hours of the morning.

I met the closeted Gavin, who owned a trucking business, and he hooked up with me. He was a very muscular, handsome man with brown hair and brown eyes. I loved the way his nose crinkled when he laughed. His laugh was contagious.

We connected the very first time we met. We were like kindred spirits, tending to spur each other on. Gavin wasn't out of the closet when we met. I was his *beard* and would be his wing man on many nights at the clubs.

We were both single and for some or other unknown reason, when we got together, we were insatiable, partying up a storm until sunrise at Club 330 in Point Road in Durban. Neither one of us knew when to call it a day. There were many nights in the VIP section when we were each other's wingman.

One Friday night, Gavin and I decided to go out and Megan asked to take her car home for her. I was going to get ready to go out with Gavin for one of our fun evenings, which did not happen.

We smelled paint while pulling up to the house. I knew Megan had bought paint and I thought she had taken it out but forgot about it. The paint tin fell over and the lid came off. When I opened the boot, the blood drained from my face. The boot looked like a milky swimming pool in a boot of her car. Gavin and I stood helpless, trying to scoop the paint out of the boot.

I called Megan to tell her what had happened. Let's just say it was like *being called into the headmaster's office.*

That evening, it was time for me to get my life together and move into my own place.

I had to get a job that paid more as I was getting very little maintenance and had to buy a house and a car as well as to furnish the house.

Within weeks, I had secured a new job, bought a house and a BMW 325i and settled in my own place with my three kids.

I was financially sound. There was no more walking on eggshells, worrying about drama that was going to erupt.

We were at peace.

Gavin and I still remain friends. He'd meet the love of his life who became his husband.

#

Out of the blue, I got a call from Tracey, my ex-sister-in-law, who had been told to get out of her house and invited her to come and live with us.

This was a whole new ball game. My ex-husband's half-sister living with me and the kids. Surprisingly, it was rather fun and she had a great sense of humour, we got along very well, and she was also a party animal.

Tracey was a tall thick-set girl with a very pretty face and loved being an aunt. The kids were terrified of her as she laid the law down, so they did not try to push the envelope when it came to her.

Tracey and I would go out some nights as a reward and paint the town red. There were lots of fun evenings going out and bonding, taking turns to look after the kids, spending time with the kids at the beach on weekends when they weren't visiting Brett.

Having Tracey as a housemate and a friend was a welcome distraction, it was someone I could share laughs with and simply be happy in the moment.

I felt happy and blessed.

I found my voice and the Tracy I knew so well.

Little did I know that another distraction was about to descend upon me, one that would change the way I saw love for the rest of my life.

Of all my favourite colours, Black and Blue are not my favourite two!
Tracy Swinson

Chapter 4
Finding My Inner Smile

Shortly before meeting Byron again, my friend/boss, Megan, and I fetched my friend Melanie from the airport as she flew in from Johannesburg to spend the weekend with me. We went straight from the airport to watch a rugby match.

On the way home while stationary at a red traffic light, we heard a loud bang and I went flying into the windscreen then chaos.

Megan jumped out of the car ran to the back of her car then looked around with her hands in the air totally confused. I got out of the car asking what had just happened, there wasn't a car behind us that was the culprit for the damage to the car. My neck was hurting so I went to sit on the side of the walkway watching Megan walk across an intersection down a side road she disappeared out of sight.

I thought to myself, *I must be dreaming but I this really happening.*

Then what I saw next had me rolling on the side walk with laughter holding onto my aching neck.

Melanie was calmly walking around the intersection picking up all her very sexy underwear off the road and tucking it into her shirt. There were G-strings, lace bras and teddy's strewn across the road. Eventually, Megan emerged cursing. She found the car that hit us, the driver was up a pole in the side road, blind drunk.

At this point, tears of laughter were rolling down our faces as Melanie approached us. The paramedics arrived and here I was in spite of the pain I was in I was trying to get the guy's number he looked like a Greek god.

When we arrived at the emergency room, they had to cut the clothes off me and told me not to move. I had fractured my C5 vertebrae they needed to stabilise it or I would have ended up a quadriplegic.

What started out as a fun evening did not end well but it was worth the laugh. Weeks in traction, I was booked out of hospital and had to wear a neck brace for four months and sustained frontal lobe damage.

When the brace came off, I was ready to carry on partying; nothing was going to stop me.

It was a hot summer evening when I was with a few friends at a club having fun, dancing the night away making up for down time, when I felt someone watching me.

I turned around, and on the edge of the dance floor stood Byron.

Byron looked better than what I remembered.

He was tall dark and handsome, with dark hair and beautiful, big brown eyes. When he smiled, it was the sexiest thing I'd ever encountered, the way he moved when he walked, the conversations we shared, felt like I was watching the ocean roll onto a shore.

As much as the sand pushed the ocean back. The waves always roll in again.

We worked together at SDS and became great friends, but unfortunately lost contact when the company closed.

Excited to see him, I ran up to him and threw my arms around him, hugging him for the longest time.

"What are you doing here?" I asked.

He stood back and looked confused, frowning, as if he was questioning what I was doing there, seeing that I was married.

I settled his mind, assuring him that I was divorced, living with my kids.

We went and had a drink and spoke for hours. We always had a connection and tonight he was looking better than I remembered.

I told him the whole story about the abuse which he told me he had suspected it but did not feel it was his place to question me. I poured my heart out to him telling of how hard it was being married to an abusive man and then leaving the way I did. I walked away with nothing and had to start from scratch. The same feeling I had the first time I met Byron was there while talking to him above the loud music I had a knot in my stomach.

I felt weak in the knees when I first met Byron, he sat in his office, laughing at *The Far Side* in the newspaper. We would share the newspaper over a few cups of coffee in the mornings, laughing. This soon resulted having lunch together, spending hours talking about life, art, and poetry. He had a way with words that would liven up a bland story with colourful nuances. I shared his joyous outlook on life, wondering what it would be like to view the world through his eyes.

Had fate brought us back together again now that I was divorced? This reunion was about to become a once in a lifetime love.

I remember one rainy day when we sat in my car, listening to music, tossing Jellybeans into each other's mouths. Every time we missed, a kiss was the forfeit.

We would meet during our lunch time at the beach and take a stroll along the shoreline with shoes in hand, talking and making jokes. We had a special connection like I had never experienced which made me question why I never had this connection with Brett when we were married. Byron and I became good friends, he was easy to talk to and he had a way that made it easy to open up to him. I guess I felt safe.

Byron and I had very similar taste in music and even though we did, he introduced me to some bands I had never heard of. For us, it was more about the lyrics to music than just the music. He loved *Coldplay* and at the time I was into the *Red-Hot Chilli Peppers* music.

Reading poetry to me with only a lit candle and soft music in the background was everything my soul yearned for.

I have never been looked at by a man, the way he looked at me, there could be a 1000 beautiful woman in a room but somehow he would look passed all of them, making me feel I was the only woman there.

Was there still a spark between us? Was it the alcohol? I thought, seeing the spark in his eyes.

We exchanged numbers and said we should make plans to see each other again. I went home that night and for the first time in a long time, I felt butterflies in my stomach.

When I woke up the following day, I could not stop thinking about Byron, toying with the idea of calling him. It felt so strange after being married to Brett and even after the divorce he was my go-to for booty calls which I had to bring to an end or what was the point in the divorce?

I sat at work staring out the window wondering what it would be like to be with a new man after seven years of marriage. Would I be good enough?

When I eventually called him, I proposed that we should meet up, he suggested that I should visit him for a coffee at his place early evening.

I arranged for Tracey to look after the kids.

I could not wait to see him. Getting ready to go meet him I did not want to make it too obvious that I was really into him so I put on a sundress, very little make-up exposing my freckles on my nose which I knew he loved and a little lip gloss. I was so nervous and excited with anticipation on the drive to his place.

When I saw him standing in his doorway, he looked exactly as I'd remembered him. Tall, dark, handsome, wearing a black fitted T-shirt and ripped jeans and barefoot. He had just got out the shower and I could smell that familiar fresh smell on him.

The butterflies returned. I felt like a schoolgirl again. Awkward.

Walking into his apartment, which was situated in a high-rise building, we settled down looking over the ocean as the sun set it was breath-taking, having a drink, our conversation flowing smoothly. Before we knew it, we stood close to each other on the balcony, staring dreamily at the moon glistening over the silvery waves.

Funny how fast time flies when you are having a good time.

Byron stood in front of me with a glass in his hand, which he then placed on the table, and looked at me, taking my face in his hands, leant in and kissed me.

I felt like I was floating. It was the most passionate soft wet kiss that left me biting my lip.

"I have been waiting so long to do that," he said in his soft velvet voice.

I looked down, then back at him, confessing, "I have been waiting all my life to be kissed like that."

With that, the kisses flowed. The attraction was so strong. Before long, he was making love to me on the floor of his apartment. He took his time to pleasure every inch of my body so gently and loving up on me like nothing I ever experienced before. The way he touched me and looked at me, making sure that I was the focus and then wanting to cuddle afterwards was a real treat.

This is mind blowing. I was married for so long and never experienced this.

Realising only much later on in my life that after I was raped, I was never comfortable in intermit moments with my husband. I always held back and never knew what an orgasm was until Byron made love to me. No fault with Brett, he was a passionate lover, he gave me three kids after all but mentally, I did not know how to receive and let go.

66

Women not having orgasms is normal, I was told but it isn't. I would highly recommend any woman lacking the above to seek out professional help, it is a mental thing not just physical.

I went home that night floating on a cloud.

When Tracey asked me how my evening went the next morning, all I could do was smile. I wanted to share every detail with her but my children where there and I wanted to hang on the very intimate pleasurable moments encountered the night before for a little longer so I could soak it all in.

During the next months, I fell head over heels in love with Byron we were soul mates. We were inseparable, spent every moment together. We connected on all levels, we were completely in tune with each other, we had a connection I had never experienced in my entire life. He was a really good artist he liked to draw and paint, and his love for literature was captivating.

We would finish each other's sentences and have long deep debates about so many different and controversial topics. Even our disagreements were sexy to the point I would get heated hand gestures flying and he would walk up to me restrain my hands behind my back with one hand and take his other hand at the back of my neck and draw me in and kiss me to stop me talking. That would end any disagreements and set a tone to dance closely with my head on his shoulder.

Tracey would look after the kids for me so I could spend more time with Byron, she would fetch and carry the kids to school if I spent the night at his house. The kids liked spending time with Tracey but also knew their boundaries with her. She was a fun aunt when she was in a playful mood and would play games with them and keep them entertained but stuck to a strict routine with them.

When Tracey spoke, the kids did not try push the boundaries like they did with me. Even after she moved out and they would give me up hill, I would tell them I am going to call your aunt Tracey and that would straighten them up until the next episode. Being a single parent is a very challenging job when you have to nurture and be the disciplinarian, too.

The kids liked Byron, he had an amazing way of telling them stories and getting their imaginations going. The kids enjoyed being around him. I did not introduce them to him until I was sure we were in a relationship.

He would also help me around the house and garden when our bodies were not intertwined.

67

One Sunday when we were alone, we spent the entire day making love, only leaving the bed to get something to drink, we twisted up the sheets all day and night long with long conversions in the dark that evening. I was exhausted.

Byron lit candles and ran me a beautiful bubble bath, picking me up and gently placing me in the bath, bathed me and washed my hair then sat back and read me poetry, we then were engaged in a long conversation.

I was exhausted and crawled into bed with wet hair, before long, I was asleep.

When I awoke up the next morning, I was late for work and quickly put on my dress and shoes, slapping on some make-up, and rushed off to work.

When I arrived at work, Mark my branch manager was the only one there. I made us some coffee and sat down in his office. He had a smirk on his face, clearly inquisitive about how my evening had gone, so I smiled.I replied, "Just fine," he grinned, leaning over his desk, looking at my legs.

I followed his eyes and looked down my leg and let out a yelp.

Byron had drawn a huge dragon up my leg with a felt tip pen while I was sleeping. I had to admit that he was a very good artist and went off to the bathroom to scrub off his masterpiece, smiling as I did so. He always did memorable little things like that with me.

He particularly loved my one toe as it had a beauty spot on it and he called that toe Marilyn Monroe.He would sketch her face in the appropriate area to highlight her best feature, then take a sheet of paper and fold it into her iconic dress, transforming it into a Marilyn Monroe-like image.

Our relationship grew into something truly wonderful, he knew how to touch my soul without even trying. I have never had such a special connection with anyone else before.

One of my favourite memories was when he met me for lunch in the poetry section of the library. He picked a book of Lord Byron off the shelf and opened it on—*She Walks in Beauty*.

She walks in beauty, like the night
Of cloudless climes and starry skies;
And all that's best of dark and bright
Meet in her aspect and her eyes;
Thus mellowed to that tender light
Which heaven to gaudy day denies.
One shade the more, one ray the less,

Had half impaired the nameless grace
Which waves in every raven tress,
Or softly lightens o'er her face;
Where thoughts serenely sweet express,
How pure, how dear their dwelling-place.
And on that cheek, and o'er that brow,
So soft, so calm, yet eloquent,
The smiles that win, the tints that glow,
But tell of days in goodness spent,
A mind at peace with all below,
A heart whose love is innocent!

By Lord Byron

I have always enjoyed the smell of a book when being opened. I got lost in the passage I was reading when Byron stood behind me pressing his body against mine, telling me not to turn round, and continued to read the poem in my ear. I could feel his breath on my neck, as the words flowed from him, closing my eyes, allowing the sound of his velvet voice to transport me to a magical world as he recited the poem to me.

When he had read the poem, he moved my hair to the side and gently kissed me on my neck. Then left.

I stood transported and transformed for a while. The kiss still lingered as I placed the book back on the shelf and ran out of the library to see if I could find him. But he was gone, nowhere to be seen. I played the moment over and over in my head through my mind all day long. He was intoxicating.

Byron had been out of work for months, so I persuaded Brett to give him a job. Byron was aware that Brett was my ex-husband and kept to himself, also not saying anything to him about us being in a relationship.

One night, one of Brett's employees saw me and Byron together and Brett made his life hell the next few weeks at work, until he let him go.

This placed unnecessary pressure on our relationship, and I felt guilty about Byron losing his job.

For the first time, Byron and I began bickering, he started displaying fits of jealousy and I played into it. I liked the way it made me feel but I know now it was not healthy.

I'd always been a party girl with an outgoing personality, which made him feel uncomfortable, not confident about the relationship we had. As he was a few years younger than me, I understood his insecurity.

Byron's insecurity affected me. I questioned if I was ready to commit to a serious relationship so soon after my divorce. He spoke about getting married which made me a little uncomfortable as I was really just enjoying what we had and what I had just found. I felt that it was too soon after getting divorced to be talking marriage. If the gap was a little longer after my divorce, I would not have hesitated. I loved Byron with my heart and soul.

Brett had moved on with his life, but he did make it impossible for me to start a new relationship with Byron, someone I fell deeply in love with.

Conflicted and confused, I had been doing so well finding my feet again, being an independent spirit. Now, I felt caged in.

One day, when Tracey was staying at her boyfriend and the kids were with Brett in Johannesburg as it was school holidays, I had to entertain our guests at a work function, which led to the evening, and we eventually all ended up at the Bourbon Street club.

While I was having a great time playing pool with Mark, my boss and our clients, I noticed that my mobile lit up numerous times. When I took the call eventually, it was Byron. He was livid that I was not home yet. I told him that I have to wait for my clients to leave and cut the call.

I wasn't surprised when I saw Byron watching me from a across the room.

I excused myself from Mark and the clients, my stomach was in knots, for the first time since leaving Brett that feeling of despair returned, rearing its ugly head.

Byron got into the car with me, not even bothering to close the door, immediately bombarding me with accusations of flirting with customers, building up a rage that resulted in him punching the windscreen in heated anger it cracked into what looked like a spiderweb. I could not help thinking if that was my face, imagine the mess.

I'd never seen so much anger in Byron, could never have imagined that it was there, but it surfaced, loud and clear.

My reaction was severe, I swung my legs round and kicked him so hard that he fell out of the car. I shut the door and drove off, watching him sit on the pavement in disbelief.

Angry and afraid, I felt heartbroken when I pulled into the driveway of the house and saw his car standing there, then did something I'd never thought I would do. I grabbed a spade and smashed the windows and side mirrors of his car. Where did all this anger come from this was not me I have never lashed out like this was not me and I did not like this person.

Sobbing myself to sleep, I would not let Byron into the house he was banging on the door and windows begging me to let him in so we could talk. I was afraid he would hurt me because that's what I grew up with and what I knew. He eventually gave up and I heard his car door shut but no engine went on. I was drifting in and out of sleep the whole night. I was more worried what my boss Mark was going to say for leaving like that and not returning to my clients.

The following morning, I found him sleeping in his car. I apologised to him for damaging his car. My heart was broken for what darkness crept up on something so amazing it was now tainted by the thing that I feared most.

When I saw the broken windscreen on my car, the realisation hit me that it could have been my face, knowing that I had to walk away from Byron, although I loved him with all my heart.

It was a drug I had to give up.

I started excluding him from my life, hoping that he would get the message, but he clung to me. Before leaving for Johannesburg that Christmas to house-sit for friend, I told him that I needed the break to give our relationship some thought.

Heartbroken during the long drive, I was tempted to turn around, but knew that I had to soldier on.

I spent a very lonely Christmas housesitting for a very good friend of mine they were going away and needed someone to feed their dogs and take care of the plants, pining to hear from Byron, speaking to him once or twice which made it more difficult, then stopped calling him until I returned home to Durban.

Eager to give our relationship another chance, and to lay down some boundaries like him giving me space when I needed it and to trust that I was not going to hurt him, so trust needed to be on the list, we agreed to meet at a pub.

When I walked up to Byron, I sensed something was wrong. His whole composure was totally different. I sensed something was up but what?

I kissed him and in that kiss, I knew he had cheated on me while I was away.

When he looked at me, I immediately sensed that he had met someone else.

"I'm sorry," he said softly.

I was heartbroken and tried to persuade him to give our relationship another chance.

"I want to have children and you can't give me that," he said, which was the hardest words anyone had ever told me.

There was nothing to negotiate or contemplate. It was over.

Devastated I left him behind as I walked to my car, tears streaming down my face, he ran after me but I was too hurt to even talk to him.

I found myself at work trying to make sense of how everything turned so quickly to him wanting children when a few weeks prior, he was happy with our little family.

Sitting at work one Friday afternoon, I needed answers to how he turned so quickly. I drove over to his place and he made me some coffee and we started to talk. I could clearly see he was still in love with me then why was he so addiment that he was done. It then dawned on me the girl he met had a hold over him and was not about to let him go. I begged him to give us a chance but he was saying no but his eyes were saying yes. I just could not fathom what it was that made him leave.

I got into my car, I turned up the music to drown out my thoughts battling to see through the tears, *No Doubt* blearing *Don't Speak* I was mouthing the words the next thing I was t-boned a car that had jumped the intersection. My car spun out of control and hit a lamppost, I immediately climbed out of the car and wandered into oncoming traffic in disbelief, I could not see out of my right eye and could feel the warm blood running down the side of my face.

I then heard a familiar voice calling to me, I turned and there Byron stood. He scooped me up in his arms and calmed me down until the paramedic took me. He said that he will check up on me and just like that, he left. Not only was my heart broken but the bones in my body too.

The next morning, he arrived at the hospital with one flower. He placed in a glass of water, telling me it was a poor man's bouquet but to me it was the most beautiful bouquet in the room. I lay there in pain with a broken hip and scapula and 20 stiches in my head and swollen back eye. He looked at me and told me I was still the most beautiful broken mess he had ever seen.

We spoke briefly not even talking about our situation when he got up to leave to go to see the new girlfriend. In that moment, I knew he was no longer my person.

It took me months to get over Byron. It was extremely difficult as we kept gravitating towards each other. Although we knew that there was no future for us, we could not stay away from each other.

I was now the other woman!

I needed to end it but did not know how. Fortunately, the woman he was seeing made it more difficult for him to see me when they moved in together.

I'd never experienced heartache like that in my life. Byron was my soulmate. I knew I would never meet anyone like him again, never love anyone like I loved him.

Our goodbye was bittersweet. We made love for the last time.

"This door is now closed," I said to him.

He looked at me and in his poetic way said, "This door will never be closed in case we find each other again."

Thank goodness for Megan.

It took copious amounts of red wine, tears, and music to get through nine months of fixing my broken heart. Every time a song we liked played, I would be reduced to tears and would need to pull the car over as to not have another accident. It was a long time before I began to feel normal again.

I was now in a good space in my life, I was healing from this broken heart and life was starting to feel good. Then while having dinner, my phone rang and the person on the other side of the phone asked me if I knew a Byron. I said yes and they asked me to come immediately.

I did not even question it. I got in my car and drove to a remote area with very dim lit building. I arrived at the security office and Byron emerged from the security office clearly shaken up. He had been hijacked earlier that day and was tied up while being driven around in the boot of his car.

Finally, when they stopped, they took him out the car and told him to kneel with a gun pushed up against his head and they pulled the trigger but the gun jammed. Byron realised what had just happened and got up and ran towards the lights he saw in the distance through a swamp arriving at the security telling them what happened the only person and number he could remember was mine.

I drove him back to his home, there was a thick silence in the drive back, I walked him into his apartment. His dad was there and said he would take Byron to open a case at the police station. I hugged him and said goodbye. Little did I know that would be the last time I would ever see him again.

I think that in the midst of all that trauma he experienced, the person he loved most was the person he reached out to. I had my answer but still walked away for my own preservation.

To this day, I am a distant friend of Byron and often think about him, smiling at the thought of him being happily married with two beautiful children. He set the bar high in terms of how to make me feel loved. I know that it was not in his nature to be violent and abusive.

Was that a one-time thing or not? I thought.

I will never know but I do know how to love.

I decided not to get involved and spent time with my children and going sporting events. I became a serial dater never allowing anything to develop beyond just friends.

No-one could measure up to Byron. I knew that.

Finding a new lease on life, I lived each day, moment by moment, soaking it all in.

I finally found my happy place and was comfortable in my own company, loving my inner smile, I did not need or want anyone in my life.

I was in love with the new me.

Life was hopeful and I was looking forward to new and exciting things that awaited me on the horizon.

New things were coming. Little did I know that a wrong number was going to change the course of my life.

Some endings are written before the beginning just like the Montague's and Capulet's!
Tracy Swinson

Chapter 5
Red Hiking Boots

On a warm summer's evening in February 2004, around 10 pm, I found myself standing in the passageway of my home, terrified, staring down the barrel of a gun.

The man who held the gun was so close to me, I could smell a mix of alcohol and tobacco on his breath. The whites of his eyes were bloodshot, gazing into my eyes. Wearing a grey T-shirt, black denims and white takkies, he motioned me to leave the bedroom, indicating that I must control my German shepherd, Anna.

I told my dog to sit and stay, fearing he would shoot her. Feeling my knees trembling, I stepped out of the room, squeezing past him. I could see the sweat glistening on his skin. He stepped closer, forcing me against the wall. I stood frozen. Although I wanted to run, my feet would not move. Every fibre of my body wanted to run but it was stuck fast to the passage floor.

A loud bang exploded as the bullet shot out of the barrel of the gun.

Everything morphed into slow motion. I saw what was happening, but could not move, feeling the bullet slam into my chest. There was no pain, only a warm sensation running from my chest to my feet as I plunged to the floor like a heap of sand.

#

A month before the shooting—when I found myself on the floor of my passageway, staring at my ceiling—I was in Cape Town on holiday with Percy.

It was a glorious day, the sun shone brightly, and a soft breeze wafted from the ocean, which was a mesmerising turquoise blue.

Standing on beach in Camps Bay, I felt the gentle spray of sea water on my face as I soaked it all in. Over my shoulder I saw the majestic Table Mountain with her Twelve Apostles.

It was a breath-taking sight, no matter how many times I'd seen this view, it never failed to amaze me. Something magical tingled inside of me when I saw it.

It was a wonderful day, Percy and I had the world to ourselves, the kids Greigan, Kyle and Nicole were with Brett while we were on holiday.

Our friends suggested that we should climb Table Mountain and take the cable-car down. It was an awesome idea, but being a fashionable big-city girl, I had not packed any suitable shoes for hiking, so I headed off to the V & A Waterfront Mall to go shopping. It probably was the worst time to be there with the mall buzzing with tourists and holiday makers shops looking bleak from the Christmas shopping just the month before.

Wandering from shop-to-shop, I eventually found a pair of hideous bright red hiking boots that I would not want to be seen dead in. They were so bright, I was sure you could see them from the moon me hiking up Table Mountain. It just did not seem practical I knew I would not wear them again.

I was excited about the prospect of my new adventure, but after much deliberation, I called the climb off as I knew I would never wear the red hiking boots other than to climb Table Mountain. So we bagged the hike for the next trip to Cape Town. I felt disappointed but there was so much more to see and do.

Little did I know that this was going to be my biggest regret to date.

As newlyweds, he wanted us to spend the rest of our holiday basking in the sun, doing some sightseeing and explore wine farms, indulge in wine-tastings before flying back to a smoggy Johannesburg.

My friends were curious about how I met Percy, marrying a man who would not adopt one, but three kids that weren't his.

"Easy, you get married first, then introduce the kids!" I joked.

One evening, Alan, a good friend of mine, invited Tracey and I for dinner. Alan was a gentle giant, blonde, with kind, blue eyes. A muscular soft-spoken Italian man armed with a great sense of humour and style.

Alan had outdone himself, beautifully setting up the table with crystal glasses and polished silverware, fit for a princess—me of course! Only to find out, many years later that he was going to ask me out that night but it was derailed by the wrong telephone number I dialled.

The evening started with a bottle of Merlot, followed by a sumptuous dinner and dessert, then more Merlot.

I suggested that we should call a few friends to join us and hastily dialled a number which I thought was my friends but wasn't. It was a number saved on my mobile which rang and rang, then went to voicemail. I cancelled the call, wondering who the number belonged to.

A few moments later my mobile rang. It was the voice from the wrong number I had dialled. Being outgoing and friendly, and having had a few glasses of wine, I was happy to chat with the stranger.

Alan and Tracey signalled that I should cut the call, but I ignored them. It could have been a stalker, but I was rather enjoying the conversation, and moved away from the dinner table to the lounge area, plopping down on the sofa, chatting away.

Twenty-minutes later, I re-joined Alan and Tracey, who were concerned about my unruly and irresponsible behaviour, worried that it could potentially have a dangerous outcome.

The caller was Percy from the wrong number I had dialled. We connected immediately and struck up a friendship, spending four months calling each other, enjoying late-night chats and laughs. For the first time since Byron left, I felt comfortable talking to Percy so openly and it felt safe flirting with someone so far away what harm could it do? Little did I know what was in store for me.

I was attracted to his quirky sense of humour. I never thought anything would develop further from our conversations strange as we were living different provinces.

When I informed him that I had three kids, he thought I was pulling his leg. Little did he know that I was being truthful, just as I discovered much later that he was a stranger to the word *truth*.

When I was on my way to Johannesburg one weekend to drop the kids off with Brett for the December holiday, Percy called me, asking what plans I had for the weekend.

I told him that it just happened that I was in Johannesburg I was dropping off my kids with their dad, but he did not believe me, inviting me to have coffee with him.

We agreed to meet up at a coffeeshop in Sandton City although we had no clue what each other looked like—those were the days before Facebook, Instagram or video calls.

Although the coffeeshop was packed, when Percy arrived very late, I was almost done with my coffee, he took no notice of anyone else and walked straight up to me.

He looked me up and down.

"So, this is you!" he said.

I was impressed. He was lucky that I did not leave as he was 20 minutes late. Normally, I would have left. I have always been a stickler for time but I had nothing planned for the evening with my friends, so I decided to watch the patrons in the coffee shop chatting away. The vibe was great and the coffee was good too, it did taste like a second cup.

Percy was slightly balding, with a good physique. I could tell by the way his T-shirt hugged his chest and arms. He was not my type looks-wise but his sense of humour was sharp and that for me was a plus. I never got weak at the knees or felt butterflies like I did with Byron and I had resigned myself to the fact there would never be another great love like that.

We hit if off straight off the bat, and sat chatting till the coffee shop closed, then moved to Midnight Owls where he chatted until the sun came up. We had knocked back a lot of shooters and by now the flirting was bouncing back and forth.

There was an amiable familiarity between us, as if we'd known each other all our lives. Percy wanted to meet up again before I went back to Durban, and we did. *The rest is history.*

We were crazy about each other and spent New Year's Eve together in Dullstroom with a good friend of his.

When we were dancing that evening with his friend Sharon, who had joined us, I remember thinking how strange it was to see him flirting with another woman across the dance floor. I wondered that maybe I was just imagining things or maybe I had had too much to drink, so I decided to overlook it.

While Percy and I were dancing, he leant in closer to me as the music was rather loud and said, "I'm going to marry you!"

I laughed. I was not going to get married again.

Well, never say never.

When I felt that it was time for my kids to meet Percy, I arranged with Brett that we would treat Greigan, Kyle and Nicole to breakfast and a movie. When we collected the kids, and when three little people hopped into the car, Percy went pale. The kids wanted to know who he was, Percy jokingly told them he was the Postman as that was the name of his business.

Later on that evening when the kids returned to Brett, Brett asked them who was this new man in my life, and all three kids replied, "Mummy is seeing the Postman." Brett was horrified and did not know how to respond to this new information.

As we drove off to Sandton, Percy was quiet. During breakfast, he excused himself and went to the bathroom. Hearing a commotion from the entrance to the nearby store, I checked up on Percy and found that he had fainted. When he gained consciousness, I suggested that we should skip the movie and go straight home.

He was a real trooper and insisted that we go to the movie. I only discovered later that Percy was recovering from glandular fever.

My son, Kyle, never warmed to Percy. Greigan and Nicole warmed to him as he had a child-like playful nature and would entertain Greigan with Spiderman comics, figurines and even dressed up one evening like Spiderman and climbed on the gate.

It was a special moment when Greigan noticed him and shouted out to Spiderman, telling him not to be afraid that he would not hurt him. Nicole was continually getting herself into mischief, and since Percy would cover for her, I didn't find out about it until much later. Since I was the stricter of the two of us, punishment didn't apply.

#

19-years later, Percy and I were in the middle of an acrimonious divorce.

All the red flags were there but when you are in love, you never see them. I guess it's true what they say about rose-tinted glasses.

On the night of my shooting, I felt unnerved and took a bath, then joined Percy on the couch to watch a movie together.

However I could, not shake of the feeling that something was very wrong. My heart was racing and my stomach was in a knot. From the age of 20, I had a specific recurring dream of me being shot perhaps this added to my anxiety that night. Things were not going well between us and I wondered if this was the reason I felt so unsettled, perhaps I just needed a good night's sleep. I realised that he did not have a successful business that he claimed to have he had serious cash flow issues. There were a number of very frightening incidents where I had to deal with thugs demanding money's owed to them. I was physically and verbally threatened by these people.

I told Percy that I was going to bed, hoping that the unsettled feeling would dissipate. Percy had a nightly routine to let the dogs out at 10 pm in the front garden, but I had asked him a few days previously to let them out into the back garden instead as I felt his routine was too predictable. But despite my request he had let the dog out into the front garden.

Before I got into that night bed, I removed my wedding rings, which was odd, as I never done this before. But for some reason that particular night it felt right and I was convinced it was because my hands felt swollen. I definitely had my angels watching over me that night.

As I settled down in bed, and was dozing off, I heard a high-pitched shrieks from the lounge, and wondered if it was Percy? As Percy opened the front door to let the dogs out four armed men stormed him and pushed him back inside the lounge. Despite his supposed prowess in martial arts and his reassurance to me that he could fight off armed assailants, he failed miserably and screamed like a child when faced with the attackers.I can only imagine how terrifying it must be being rushed by four armed men at once, he never spoke about his trauma from that night. I could only imagine how emasculated he felt and helpless not being able to protect his wife and step-children.

Although I kept calm and quiet, I took a bullet in the chest. I will never understand why I was shot, I was no threat to anyone.

Laying on the floor with my kids whom I thought were fast asleep in their beds, I heard Percy speaking calmly to the perpetrators.

Fear gripped me, it felt like a python had coiled around me, suffocating me. I was gasping for air.

I thought about how it was possible that this could have happened. One reads about it in the newspaper, hear it on the news, or see it in many movies and TV shows. Not in a million years did I ever expect that my family would become a statistic.

An overwhelming feeling of vulnerability hit me as I lay helpless in the passageway, not being able to move my arms or legs. As a mother, my instinct was to protect my children with my life but my body would not move.

All I could think was, '*I should have climbed Table Mountain in those hideous red hiking boots,*' realising that I might never be able to scale that magnificent wonder. Looking ridiculous for a moment is better than a lifetime of regret.

I decided that if I made it out alive, I would live my life with no regrets. Life is precious, too short to keep stalling and leave things for tomorrow.

One never knows what tomorrow holds.

My daughter cried out to me. She must have been woken when the gunshot went off.

I desperately tried moving my legs, trying to manoeuvre my arms to leopard crawl to her, but I couldn't move, I could not even move a finger.

I teared up realising that I was totally helpless. Completely defenceless.

I called to my daughter, instructing her to stay in her room and not come out. I kept consoling her, telling her to keep calm, praying that she would follow my orders.

At this stage, I had no idea how many intruders there were in the house, all I heard was muffled voices and multiple bodies darting back and forth.

One of the perpetrators kept going in and out of my daughters' room, he took one step forward, then one step back, as if something kept pushing him out of the room. I remember telling this man there was nothing of value in that room little did they know one of my biggest treasured lay frightened and I could not get to her.

I was terrified for her, pleaded with God to spare my family, take my life instead. If he spared our lives, I would do my best to be a better person.

Can one negotiate with God? I had nothing to lose.

As I lay in the passageway staring up at the ceiling, I looked at the lightbulbs, thinking that we needed to change it, they were so bright, it actually blinded me. There was this warm comforting feeling engulfing my body and I thought how strange I feel like this while this horrendous crime was in procession.

Why was I even concerned about the lights?

Men trampled over me as if I was dirty laundry, stealing our belongings, carrying it away lock, stock, and barrel.

If anyone needed a speedy house removal team, these men would be doing great business, I thought. It is strange that in dire moments like this such arb thoughts cross one's mind.

I felt euphoric.

Is this what it feels like when you are dying? I thought. I remembering this conversation with my pops asking him if it hurt when you die, well I guess I was about to find out I thought to myself.

I battled breathing, but I was not ready to die yet, desperately clasping on to my conscious so that I could protect my kids, make sure that no harm would come to them.

Slipping in and out of consciousness, I came round when a man hit my head with the butt of the gun.

"Don't look at my face," he said. "Where is the second set of car keys?"

I closed my eyes not to aggravate him any further. He was a bulky man, reeking of booze, sweat and cigarettes. He did not know that I could not see him as I was blinded by the lights above my head.

I told him to look on the ledge above the recipe books to find the set of keys in the kitchen.

I suddenly panicked and could not breathe although I kept telling myself to stay calm. I knew this was serious. I lay there desperately fighting to breath while telling myself to stay calm.

Keep your thoughts clear. I thought to myself.

I heard Percy calmly telling them where they could get what they were looking for. Percy told me later that they'd kicked him in the head, breaking his nose, leaving him lying face-down, tied down, with blood pouring out of his nose.

Percy's blood was running out of his body while my lungs were filling up with blood. It is amazing that a small piece of metal can change the whole trajectory of your life in a split second. Quite often, people refer to guns being dangerous but I think it is the person holding the gun.

I could hear myself telling my daughter Nicole to stay in her bed. These men were on a high and edgy. Ruthless. I did not want them to shoot her when she got in their way.

Greigan was fast asleep, nothing could wake him. Kyle was awake in his wisdom, after hearing the gunshot, grabbed his brother out of his bed and moved him to his own bed. At this stage, Greigan had woken up, and Kyle had told his little brother to pretend that he was sleeping.

Kyle wisely did not move, watching silently through half-closed eyes as the men plundered their room, robbing their treasured television and PlayStation games.

The man who shot me kept a close eye on me. He knelt and spread my legs wide open, shifting closer to me, ripping off my shorts, then shoved his fingers inside of me. He leant forward, his salivating face inching closer to mine, his foul, boozy breath drowning me.

I knew I was going to relive this monstrous nightmare for the rest of my life if I made it out alive.

Consciously crippled and powerless, I was unable to defend my humanity. I could not do anything to fight off the monster.

Tears ran down my face as I expected the worst to happen, knowing that I could not feel anything, that I would be lifeless to the brutality of him raping me.

The only pleasant thought that swam through my muddled thoughts were that it was I who was going to be severely violated, and not my innocent Nicole.

At least, through all the horror of the brutal onslaught, there was at least one thing to be grateful for.

Then, another gunshot blasted as one of the men tried to shoot our adorable bearded Colley, but thankfully missed.

I could hear our neighbours rallying as one of the men pulled up outside our house in a White BMW and hooted. Another man made a dash for it with our CD rack, dropping it clumsily, with CDs crashing on the concrete, then dropped everything and bolted.

At this point, the man that was about to rape me jumped up and ran out the house with his pants being pulled up while sprinting out the house.

Our 20-minute ordeal felt like aeons. It was over just like that, leaving a trail of broken, damaged, traumatised family.

Percy managed to untie his hands and was calling the police when our neighbours Ilidio and Estelle entered the house, telling him that they had also alerted the police and called for an ambulance. I will never understand how he managed to untie himself and make it to me before my kids did?

Percy and the kids ran over to me and when they saw me laying there, I told them that I had no feeling in my arms and legs.

I told Percy that I had been shot, he told me he thinks I am just in shock. He could not see any gunshot wound. On closer inspection, he saw the hole in my nightgown with gunpowder residue around the hole, realising that the gun had been so close to my skin that it cauterised the hole.

Greigan stood confused as he watched Nicole bring me a pillow, resting my head on it, sitting close to me, with Kyle covering me gently in a blanket.

#

I had no idea how badly injured I was internally, it felt as if I was being sucked under water in a strong current that pulled me into a silent darkness.

No matter how desperately I tried to escape, I was pulled into an abyss, as if I was swimming against a tide in the ocean that was much stronger than me. I had no choice but to surrender. I fought so hard to break away from this force that was drowning me, I needed to come up for some air.

Faces and voices around me faded. As I gasped for air, I could feel myself panicking, but I was helpless and could not stop what was happening to me.

Then silence descended.

The bullet ruptured my lung, my spine. I could not breath. Lost consciousness.

If this was death, it is serene.

#

When the ambulance arrived, they had problems lifting me into the gurney. Our neighbour and Percy assisted getting me onto the gurney carefully. I was rushed to Life Clinic.

The doctor told Percy to contact my parents. They were not sure if I was going to make it through the night.

Through the thick blanket of silence, I recall hearing my mum's voice telling me to 'fight'. To this day, I am not sure whether it was real or simply my imagination.

It was ironic. My mum was also fighting for her life. Diagnosed with breast cancer and undergoing treatment, she had her own battle to conquer. The champion she had always been, she vigilantly watched over me, cheering me on. A mother's love is indeed unconditional as I realised later that her own situation she knew she was dying but was by my side making sure I would live giving me words of comfort and encouragement to not give up. She was selfless like this always put others before herself.

Mum told me that Percy assisted the doctors in the ER to cut the clothing from my limp body, they'd rush to get me to the MRI, trying to keep my blood pressure stable.

I was not conscious during the crazy rush to save my life. All I recall was waking up briefly, asking people around me to help me, complaining that I could not breathe.

Then darkness and silence swallowed me.

The doctors informed Percy that the next 24-hours were critical. They were unsure that I was going to make it as I had lost too much blood having received four pints it was going to be a wait and see moment. They did not remove the bullet as they rarely do in spinal cord injury. Fortunately, the bullet was trapped under my scapula. The next 24 hours were critical.

#

What Nicole recalled from that tragic evening…

"I remember this day like it was yesterday. It was a Thursday night I was being difficult, refused to go to bed, just wanted to stay up with my mum and watch Desperate Housewives. She eventually put me to bed.

A loud bang woke me from a nightmare I was having. I was not sure what I heard spilt from my dream or whether it was real.

There were murmurs sounding from the house. Stuff shuffling.

When the second gunshot blasted, I knew that something was terribly wrong. Filled with fear, I called for my mum, wanting to go to her.

"Just stay there, Nix," I heard her say seriously in her big mummy voice. "Everything will be all right. Don't get out of bed. Stay there!"

It was then that a tall, skinny man rushed into my room and looked me in the eyes.

"Hush, sweetie pie, it will all be over soon."

I could not move and was frozen with fear. Although I was gripped by an intense cold, I was sweating profusely.

I just wanted my mum but knew I couldn't get to her. From my bed, all I could see slightly into the hallway, were a pair of feet. I wasn't sure if it was my mum or oldest brother Kyle's feet, but I just lay waiting for these men to leave our house.

Hours and hours flashed before my eyes in seconds.

Then I heard the car tyres screech, driving away from our house.

When we got the okay from Percy, we jumped from our beds and rushed into the passageway.

That's when I saw my mum lying helplessly in the passage with a big black hole in her robe. She was shaking and I immediately ran back to my room to grab a blanket to cover her and get her warm.

I don't know how I knew but I just knew she was in shock and needed to be kept warm.

A few moments later, our house was filled with unfamiliar faces. People crowded me. Talking to me, but I couldn't even hear them.

I was still confused at what had really happened.

Will I see my mum again?

The ambulance had rushed her down the road to Rose Acres Hospital. A few moments later, Percy had run back from the hospital to come check on us and let us know my mum will be okay but he really didn't know at that point if she was or not.

My Gran had arrived to fetch us and take us all back to her house.

I sat up till the sun came up to hear if my mum was okay. I did not sleep a wink that night.

#

Gregian's memory of the evening...

"All I can remember is that I thought the Gardener had come to play PlayStation."

87

Kyle's recall of the evening…

"It was a warm humid Thursday evening, I went to bed but could not sleep and was thinking how I could get out of going to school the next day.

I heard my mum say good night to Percy. He carried on watching a movie. I heard him get up to let the dogs out before locking up to go to bed.

Then I heard a noise like a rush and a very loud thump. I assumed something was happening.

I then heard Percy say what do you want and take what you need but please don't hurt anyone. That's when I realised there were people in our house to rob us. I heard these guys grabbing stuff and taking it to our car. I told myself to stay calm, my immediate concern was if my little brother, my sister and my mum and Percy were okay.

My door looked onto my mum's room and my sister's.

I grabbed Gregian out of his bed and told him to lie still and pretend to be sleeping. We lay back-to-back while I faced the door and kept my eyes slightly closed enough to see what was going on.

One of the guys went into my sister's room and walked out.

I then heard a gunshot—it was meant for our dog but missed.

Then a guy came into our room put the gun in his back pocket then helped himself to our TV and PlayStation.

There was a moment I thought about grabbing the gun and shooting him but there were a lot of unknowns.

I was watching my mum's room and saw her step out and a guy pointing a gun at her. The gun jerked forward with a loud bang. I saw my mum falling down in slow motion to the floor like a tree being cut down.

That is when it got real, and the worry hit me. She wasn't moving or saying anything. That's when I heard Percy tell them that the cops were coming, and the neighbours were on their way.

They then left!

I ran to my mum, and she said, "I can't feel my legs and can't breathe."

I put a pillow under her head and my sister put a blanket over my mum.

Percy called for ambulance and police. Our neighbours came to assist us.

The police took statements. We then went to Percy's mum.

This wasn't a day for school.

Have no regrets. Live today like there is no tomorrow because who knows what tomorrow holds so dance in the rain, feel the grass under your feet and do what you can with the precious time you have.

\-   T Swinson

Chapter 6
My Life My Fight

When I awoke during the early morning hours, it felt like a truck was parked on my chest. I could not move, my arms or my body I felt pinned down like a magnet to a fridge.

I heard someone shuffling next to my hospital bed and wanted to tell the person that I was okay, forcing my eyes open, only seeing the ceiling and the lights above me.

"Can you hear me, Mrs Swinson," a voice asked, and I blinked.

It was the nurse, who rushed out of the ward to call the doctor.

I slipped back into a warm stream of darkness.

I awoke to the welcoming sight of Percy who stood next to my hospital bed, informing me that I had been transferred to the Neuro ICU in Milpark Hospital.

He was discussing my case with a neurosurgeon, looking rather serious at the X-Rays the doctor held.

I looked at the tubes coming out my ribcage and central line into my chest, hooked up to monitors that purred and beeped to the beat of my heart.

What is happening? I thought. It still felt as if a truck was parked on my chest.

When Percy noticed I was conscious, he immediately paid all his attention to me and with poker face "You will be fine," he said.

I was grateful to hear those words. At that point, I would have taken any answer, except someone telling me that I was not going to live. In his state of denial or wisdom not sure which of the two but him telling me I was going to be fine, allowed me not to be put in a box or to be labelled the words you will never walk again has not yet been whispered to me yet so in my mind, this was only temporary.

I stopped asking questions. It was obvious that I was in a serious condition as I could not move my limbs. I fully realised that there was a massive struggle that lay ahead and that I needed to be stronger than I have ever been before to survive the ordeal and leave the ICU.

The set up in Neuro ICU was well designed and organised the nurse station was in the middle of the unit overlooking all the patients and the beds that were laid out in a circle around the nurse station so at any given time they could have eyes on all patients there were only 10 beds in the Neuro ICU. Their phone rang constantly which was extremely unnerving for me and I could never tell why until later.

My heart melted when my kids walked up to me. Seeing their beautiful faces, knowing that they were alive, is all a mother could ever ask for. I could see the trauma in their faces, the relief and happiness in their eyes just to see me alive is something that will remain in my heart forever. No child should ever be exposed to this kind of heinous crime.

They were traumatised, but happy to see me. In no time, they were chatting up a storm, they told me that were staying with a friend of Percy's, who spoilt them rotten.

Everyone was trying their utmost best to make up for the horrendous torture they endured during that tragic night, supporting the kids through their trauma counselling.

It was the best, blessed gift I could have ever received when the kids visited me, inspiring me to fight even harder to get out of the ICU. No-one truly knows the value of family until you are in a situation that led me to this Neuro ICU.

One afternoon I asked Percy if he could please change the light bulbs in the passage because they were too bright. He looked at me for a moment then told me that they had not worked in months. I insisted that they did work, then I realised that the light was not the passage light it was something far brighter and it brought comfort in that dire moment.

A few weeks later, the tube that was in my lung was removed and I was able to breathe properly again. As the intercostal muscles on my ribcage were paralysed and they could not expand and contract, I had to learn how to breath from the bottom of my diaphragm. The breathing exercises became a daily routine and taught me how to breathe properly without any difficulty.

There were many challenges I had to overcome in the ICU. The most startling test was stabilising my blood pressure. Whenever the nurses sat me up, I passed out. They really battled to get a proper blood pressure reading.

I had the nursed running on many occasions when they could not get a pulse after I passed out, after a while they were like hawks watching me and monitoring me very carefully. I don't think their hearts could take any more scares like they had with me.

It worsened to such an extent that they called in the assistance of a cardiologist, who placed me on an adrenalin drip, attempting to increase my blood pressure. This was not successful, I became addicted to the adrenalin, I loved the buzz it gave me even though it did nothing for my low blood pressure and it took a week for the nurses and doctor to wean me off it. I would go into fits of panic whenever I became aware of them lowering my dosage.

One evening, they sedated me and weaned me off the adrenalin during my sleep.

When I awoke the next morning and realised that the drip was disconnected, I panicked, dreading having to constantly lose consciousness. It never made any difference whether I was conscious or unconscious, I was addicted to the boost it gave me.

Not being able to turn myself, I had to be turned every four hours in order not to develop any pressure sores. It was difficult to turn me while I was connected to monitors and tubes coming out of my rib cage so I could not lie on my right side. Shortly after my tube was removed, Miriam, my assigned nurse, discovered a huge pressure sore on my sacrum. They dressed it and had a wound specialist clean and dress it but it just got worse.

Eventually, they had a plastic surgeon come look at it. After two weeks of dressing it, he warned the staff and me that lying on my back it not a good idea. Today, I still do not sleep on my back but in a foetal position with a pillow between my legs. Little things I enjoyed like sleeping with socks on in winter was a thing of the past, when I discovered that caused pressure sores too, there is so much we take for granted.

The ICU nurse that was assigned to me was Miriam, a short, plump lady with slightly greying hair whose smile always lit up the room.

I had some days where everything ran smoothly, but mostly endured the hardship of trying my best to cope with the physical obstacles that challenged me.

During my sleep one evening, my blood pressure plummeted drastically. As Miriam and the nurses battled to raise my blood pressure, I felt myself slipping into a dark abyss.

I struggled to breathe the following morning and had a wet cough. By late afternoon, my lung had collapsed again. Miriam and the neurosurgeon had to reopen the space between my ribcage, inserting a tube to drain the water off my lung. I was fully conscious during the procedure.

This set-back threw me into a downward spiral.

When Miriam arrived the following morning, she was disappointed to that I had not eaten and refused to do physio.

She gently took my hand and said in a soft tone, "If you want to leave this hospital alive, you need forgiveness in your heart. You must forgive the men who did this to you."

I stared at her in utter disbelief.

How could she even think to say something like that to me? Could she not see what they had done to me? Grasp what they stole from me?

Miriam's wise words swam around in my head.

Although I was still facing obstacles, and fighting for my life, two weeks later I decided to forgive *them*. To never again look at what had happened in anger or bitterness.

That was the day when my eyes opened, when I started to see the tiniest of changes in my life, changes I welcomed and embraced with an open heart.

I was alert and agile when the police detective took my statement, talking him through the events that occurred. He made his notes. Not once did he look at me, which I thought was rather odd. When he got up and left still looking down at the floor, I realised that the hospital gown had slipped down, and my well-rounded breasts were exposed. I giggled to myself thinking that poor man.

After my statement was done, he informed me that the perpetrators were in custody. It was a breakthrough case for the police, the men formed part of a large syndicate. He told me that when the police searched the house for evidence, a stranger in the township found my purse in a dustbin and reported it to the bank.

The bank contacted the police station and they then followed the lead. From there they raided all the hotspots in the township the perpetrators frequented, uncovering more than what they expected.

I was relieved that these dangerous criminals were apprehended and that they would be held accountable for their ruthless actions.

Soon after the investigator left, Miriam plonked a breakfast tray in front of me, with eggs, bacon, tomato and mushrooms and toast on the side. Miriam turned and left the room not like every other day where she would help feed me today was different, she left me to figure it out myself.

I was starving and reached for my knife and fork, discovering to my dismay that it was difficult to use my hands the way I used to. Feeling frustrated, I pushed the breakfast tray away from me using my arm.

The loud crash of the tray as it hit the floor briefly roused the attention of the nurses, who gave it one look and continued with their tasks.

Miriam rushed over to the bed and dutifully cleaned up the mess. Without saying a word, she finished the task and left.

I called her and reprimanded her for giving me the tray of food, knowing that I could not use my hands properly.

She ignored my harsh attack and left, returning a half-an-hour later with a plate of five slices of toast, butter, and a knife.

"If you are really hungry, you will find a way to get the butter on the toast," she huffed and put the plate in front of me, then marched off.

I sat there for while in absolute disbelief, trying for 15 minutes trying to pick up the knife, then eventually used my index finger to smear butter on the toast. There were crumbs and butter all over the place but two hours later I called her to inspect my handy work.

"You are ready to do physio on your hands," Miriam smiled. "Let's get them working again."

And so, the task began of reviving my hands.

#

My mum and I shared the same birthday. It was miraculous that she and my dad brought my kids to the ICU to celebrate my 35th Birthday.

My mum visited me regularly after finishing chemotherapy for her breast cancer. She did not look well, although she reassured me that she was doing well. All the time she visited me, the conversations between us were on a very deep level and her telling me that life is worth fighting for.

Some days, she was incoherent and nothing she said made any sense, but she did prepare me for what was to come 'her death' in her own way without me realising it she would bring personal items of hers and ask me to give it to the kids to remember her by. At the time, I thought it odd but today it made perfect sense. My children have kept what she gave them and have treasured each gift as a remembrance of their nurturing grandmother.

My brother-in-law, Jude and his boyfriend snuck Moet Chardon, cheese, and biscuits into the ICU to celebrate my birthday.

Jude had his own unique way of dressing and liked the attention he got. Gifted in hairdressing, he was a fun but tortured soul and had a lot of problems with drugs and authority. His father did not accept him nor did his brother Percy until about two years ago. I was very close to him. We were insatiable when we were together. I really loved him to bits, and it broke my heart when things did not work out the way it should have between Percy and me.

They poured the champagne into paper cups so no-one could see what we were sipping. It was the most fun I had since I settled in ICU.

We laughed like naughty school children, chatting, passing visiting hours. The welcome distraction was short lived until Miriam arrived, informing us that Dr Snyckers was on his way, warning me that he was a solemn, grumpy old man who never smiled.

The first thing Dr Snyckers questioned was why the ward was smelling of alcohol.

I fibbed, telling him that it was my birthday, and that my brother-in-law was visiting, he had a bit if a drinking problem. He glared at me from above his wire rimmed glasses.

I'm sure he did not believe me for one second, he'd heard many such whoppers, but he chose to ignore it, never mentioning it again.

Jude was a loud eccentric and gifted me a makeover as a birthday gift. He arrived with all his hairdressing equipment, bossing the nurses around like they were minions working at his salon, who became his assistants, putting foils into my hair, blow-drying it.

All I could really do was just lay there and enjoy every minute of their pampering.

He did a fabulous job. It's truly amazing how getting one's hair done make you feel like a queen. I was extremely grateful for his thoughtful treat.

When you are cooped up in an ICU ward for three months, you get a lot of time to think about the meaning of life. The one thing I never questioned was why it had to happen to me. I certainly pondered why I was spared, and what the purpose was of me being there.

At 9:30 pm one night, a huge commotion erupted outside the ICU ward. The nurses rushed to find out what caused the disruption.

Miriam arrived and told me that there was a woman who demanded to see me immediately.

I had no TV and was as bored as hell, so I thought it would be great to have some company.

I greeted Lizl, a petit, short mousy brown-haired woman wearing spectacles, who sat down next to my bed, and burst out in tears when she looked at me.

Did I make her cry? I thought to myself. This was awkward, I felt uncomfortable and incredibly vulnerable.

Lizl told me that she'd gotten off work and decided that she was going to take her life. After running a bath for herself, she opened a capsule of pills and poured herself a whiskey. She was adamant to end feelings of feebleness and futility. She had not been happy for very long time. No-one understood her suffering.

Waiting for her bath to fill up, she had the urge to down more pills, drink her whiskey and read the newspaper for the last time. She looked at the tablets sprawled across the table, then cast her eye on an article in the newspaper about my shooting and what I endured.

Without thinking, she grabbed her car keys and drove straight to Milpark Hospital.

I was lost for words as I listened to Lizl's story and could not relate to what she went through, something I was not familiar with: *Depression.*

I'd always been under the impression that depression was a lonely man's disease. No-one could fathom the anguish or pain the person dealt with and did not how to approach the person or how to console them.

Lizl spoke for ages about her life and the darkness she'd live with on daily basis.

I wondered if she had ever sought professional help, knowing that during those days anti-depressants was a taboo and frowned upon by society.

I asked her if she thought about getting professional help.

How ironic, I thought, here I was trying to make sense of my own life, figuring out ways to find the path forward, and consoling a young woman on how to fight for her right to be alive, to claim her place in the world.

Words are cheap until you have to one day do exactly that!

We shared a hearty laugh when I told her of that horrid night I was shot, it was my way of coping, keeping things light. I stayed in touch with Lizl after rehab but never heard from her again. Looking back at that situation I was a broken mess and here my story had a positive impact on a complete stranger's life.

I found myself trying to inspire the people around me in the ICU ward because the nurses give so much of their lives and never talk about their struggles, so I decided to bring joy rather than a statistic they were taking care of.

My own demons were being attended to despite everything going on around me.

After the police released my statement, I received many visitors I'd never imagined. My support system was extensive.

A highlight was when Megan, a friend who felt like home to me, visited me shortly after the shooting incident. It was exactly the support I needed to lift my spirit, inspired me to be positive and push harder, getting me out of the grey ICU ward.

#

Megan's recall:

I was so shocked when I got the call from Percy's mum that my best friend had been shot. It broke my heart to see my friend lying there in that state.

I found it upsetting that she was shot, being a woman who posed no threat to anyone.

Why? I sat with Percy in the coffee shop asking him about questions of the that awful evening but no matter what he said it just did not make any sense why would my friend get hurt like this?

#

Dr Snyckers was a very serious man, who took himself seriously and never smiled.

As a friendly outgoing person, I adore seeing the smiles on people's faces. I was adamant to make Dr Snyckers smile, at least once, if only faintly before I left the ICU.

I asked Percy to bring my green furry monster slippers to the ward. He had no idea what I was up to, but when I told him of my plan to frighten the living daylights out of Dr Snyckers, he was as keen as mustard.

Before Dr Snyckers did his rounds the following morning, I asked Miriam to help me get the monster slippers on to my feet.

When Dr Snyckers arrived, I tearfully complained bitterly about how swollen my feet was, how off colour they were.

He stared at me solemnly at me and simply nodded, drawing the curtain, and whipped back the covers.

Dr Snyckers jumped with fright, letting out a gentle yelp, until realising that it was only slippers. To my disbelief, he roared with laughter, to such an extent that Miriam and the nurses rushed in to watch the spectacle. They'd also never seen him cackle and stared at him in awe.

I too, smiled.

Mission accomplished. He was human after all.

The three months I spent in ICU had some comic relief. Although things went wrong, I found humour in it.

One morning, I was told that they were going to change my bed as it wasn't working properly. I laughed, imagining them flinging me out of the bed, and shrugged, giggling. I was still hooked up to monitors, drips, and drains when the porters arrived with a new bed. I was unprepared for what was about to happen. They positioned the bed next to mine and explained that they were going to move me across.

When they pushed the button to lower the bed, the bottom half of the bed collapsed. I went flying, hanging from the drip and monitor cables, and even lost my hospital robe. I laughed so loud that Miriam and the nurses joined in, still recovering from the shock and the damage that could have been done. While I was flung from my bed hanging on by the monitor wires, I screamed out loud "Bungy!" The nurses all burst out laughing when they realised, I was fine and the only word I could find was 'Bungy'.

Any shred of dignity dissipated with the comic events that occurred when I was in ICU, especially if you are incapacitated to the extreme, where not even your tummy could work without assistance. *It was go big or go home for me.*

After a nurse gave me a laxative, she would switch shifts. If I did not know any better, I thought this was a cruel joke she played on the next nurse, who would arrive and find that I had soiled myself and was in need of help. What was to come, neither of us expected. When she drew the curtains and whipped back the bedding, everything that was once in my bowel, was flung across the room, on the curtains and even all over the nurse.

With no dignity left, I could only laugh at the expression on her face. She slipped on the mess that was on the floor and had no choice but to sit in it and join me in the laughter. I did feel bad for her as she spent the rest of the afternoon cleaning up the mess while I just lay there. I could not help myself and let out a giggle every now and then.

The one thing I was grateful for was that being in a Neuro ICU, all except for one patient, the rest were brain dead and on life support.

In the midst of our hysterical laughter, the phone rang off its hook.

Nurses scrambled back and forth to another patient's bedside and back to the phone. Miriam told me that this patient was an organ donor and that his organs were desperately needed to save another person's life.

The nurses had to be tolerant and wait for the patient's family to decide when the life support should be terminated. It was like vultures that hovered, waiting for an opportune moment to swoop down and harvest what was needed to save another life. It was similar to the law of equivalent exchange, where something had to be lost to be gained. To me, it was not a win-win situation.

With all the madness that was going on around me and in my mind, I realised that my husband was not going to step up to the plate and be a provider. I started to panic when this gut feeling set in. I knew that it was going to be difficult to get a job and needed to reconsider my future career options.

My manager from DHL visited me a week later. Paul told me that they created an opportunity for me in training. I was very grateful but could not see me doing it as a job. I did not know how mobile I would be when I left the ICU and told him that I was not capable of making any decisions yet.

"You can at least find us a salesperson," Paul said tongue-in-cheek.

I smiled at him and accepted the challenge. What possessed me, I have no idea when I replied, "15 percent and we have a deal."

Paul agreed and I went straight to work, laying on my back, barking out orders for adverts to be placed, outlining the criteria. I even got Percy to take a look at some of the CVs.

I selected three strong candidates and recommended them for the sales position. Within two weeks, one of them were secured and I made my first sixty-thousand grand, resting on my back in ICU. This is how I launched my own company Khula Placements from my ICU bed.

I had become family to the nurses and staff. Even the chef visited me and asked what I wanted for breakfast and lunch. It could be anything off the menu and even included some sushi that he had especially delivered for me. A good meal was always welcome, especially if you had all those hours waiting patiently for the next physio session.

I made friends with Ettien, a young man who had also been involved in a shooting accident and was paralysed from the waist down. He had a delightfully playful nature and was up and about before me, then left for rehab. Shortly after he left, I was released from ICU and placed in a private ward.

I was overjoyed to be out of ICU and knew that everything was going to be well.

I settled comfortably in my new room. I had a photograph of my kids next to my bed, staring at me.

I was able to wear T-shirts and leggings and took trips to the coffee shop on the floor below.

I was still not able to sit up straight without passing out, so I had to be tipped back in the wheelchair to prevent this from happening, but it never prevented me from going for a cup of coffee.

I could receive visitors during visiting hours and always looked forward to seeing my kids and parents.

For the first time since I arrived at Milpark Hospital, I finally had someone come see me that was an inspiration for me to fight and not give up.

Miss South Africa 1991, Dianna Tilden-Davis was attacked by a hippopotamus in Botswana in Africa while on holiday. She was at the hospital getting her wounds checked out and heard about my ordeal. When she was done with her appointment and visiting the staff that took care of her, she came to give me a word of encouragement and left a book for me called *I Have Life.*

She told me that it doesn't matter how bad things look. The key is to fight back and stay positive. It was refreshing having someone that had a traumatic experience and knew what it felt like to face a battle that is life changing like mine and to give words of encouragement. I felt a new sense of hope and gusto to take on whatever life offered me next.

The book she gave me brought me much encouragement in the story of a woman whom survived rape and attempted murder and was left for dead, her will to live she crawled from the bushes holding her intestines in with her shirt and kept her head down to hold it in place as all the muscles in her neck were cut and she had no control over the movement of her head as she crawled to a highway to get help. She had two choices to lie down and die or to crawl to find help and live. Sometimes, life is that simple you can fight or not.

A week after leaving ICU, my mum and dad visited me, she had completed her chemotherapy and was waiting on her appointment with the oncologist.

While I was talking to my mum, I could see that everything was not in order, there was something wrong.

My mum found it hard to tell me the story of how Bruce Lee was paralysed and walked again. She became very frustrated when she could not find the right words to tell me the complete story. She could not remember Bruce Lee's name and kept telling me that Chinese man, I could see my dad was getting agitated and impatient with her because she was unable to recall certain words. My dad kept telling her to shut up and she turned to him and said "You shut the fuck up you silly cunt!"

I had never heard my mother swear like that ever and wondered if she had spoken her mind more often perhaps she would not have got cancer. She was good at bottling things up.

Her cancer had spread to her brain, and she was not very compos mentis, mumbling incoherently about how Bruce Lee broke his back and pushed himself, believing that he would walk again. She tried to tell me to not give up and have faith. That walking again was a possibility.

There it was, that 1%. That maybe, the doctors got it all wrong?

Two days later, she suffered a stroke and was admitted to hospital. I lay in my hospital bed and felt helpless, disconnected from my mum. I just wanted to be by her side and hold her hand, comfort her with the thought that someone was there.

The following day around 10 am, Miriam visited me and told me that my mum had passed away that morning. I sobbed uncontrollably. Nothing she said could stop the pain and loss I felt. I realised this was not the time to fall apart so I dried my eyes and put on a brave face in hope of keeping the rest of my life together.

When Percy arrived, I gathered myself. He told me that he would sneak me out of the hospital to see my mum. He helped me get dressed and fetched a wheelchair, then informed the nurses that we were going downstairs for a coffee. He wheeled me straight to his father's car as he did not have a car and my car had been stolen during the robbery.

I was happy to see my kids waiting in the car for me.

We drove to the Johannesburg General Hospital and made our way to the ward.

Percy told the kids that they could not come with us and wheeled me up to the bed where my mum was still laying. I was numb I didn't know what I was feeling if it was relief or grief, I just knew she was no longer going to suffer. My dad and gran were there.

I was angry at my dad that he was not at my mum's side when she suffered through the night and passed away. Fortunately, my gran was there, holding her hand when she passed.

The nurses had swaddled her in a sheet. Only her face was visible. She looked so beautiful. Even in death, she had an angelic smile on her face and looked peaceful. I was relieved that she had been released from her painful torment and was no longer suffering in silence.

I slipped my hand under the sheet and placed my hand on her arm. She was still warm. I sat in silence for what seemed like eternity. I glanced out of the window and saw that the sky had turned a spectacular burnt orange, which was very unusual.

Then I felt my dad's hand on my shoulder I did not acknowledge him I was angry at him for not being at her side when she passed.

I was numb after taking another loss.

Percy wheeled me out of the ward and straight back to the car where the kids waited patiently.

When I was back in my hospital bed, I sat in silent disbelief. I could not fathom how it had only been eight months ago when she was diagnosed with cancer, and now was gone.

I got permission to attend my mum's funeral but cannot remember much of it as I was heavily medicated, which suppressed my emotions.

I sat in my wheelchair, tipped back so that I would not pass out.

I could vaguely see Mum's coffin out of the corner of my eye. I did not want to see it because I would then know that it was real and my mum was no longer with me.

I stared out into the distance and drifted a million miles away. All I could think of was my mum and who I was going to call when I needed her.

My mum was buried under the soil. She deserved much more. There was no eulogy, the church was packed to capacity I never realised how many people loved my mum. The pastor of the church invited people in the congregation to come up and say something in memory of my mother, an hour later I realised how many lives she touched with her kindness.

After the service, I was wheeled back to the hospital.

One day followed the other and my physiotherapy progressed. They prepared me for rehab and taught me how to catheterise.

I thought about how my life had spiralled into a new normality. How we take the simplest things like urinating for granted. I became conscious of how precious time was. Every four hours, I had to take precaution in order not to have an accident, which happened often as my mind had not aligned with my body's new way of functioning.

The time I spent in ICU was nothing, I could have ever imagined, that I not only had to fight for my own life, but for the lives of my children too.

It would have been easier to give up hope but being stubborn is sometimes a blessing.

I was not prepared to go out like this under any circumstances, no matter how insurmountable the obstacles were. It would be on my own terms.

I thought the battle was over, little did I know that it was merely the beginning of a race for years to come, let alone what awaited me the following day.

We have two choices in life; live or die.
Tracy Swinson

Chapter 7
Broken Body but Not My Spirit!

The big day arrived. I was ready to leave Milpark Hospital.

I graduated to rehab where I got to learn how to live the new norm in a body that is broken.

Percy and I pulled up at the rehabilitation centre and everything in me screamed, '*No!*'

We parked in front of the dull, greyish building, with all its wheelchairs lined up at the entrance. I sat in the car waiting for Percy and my heart just sank I was not ready for this I needed a breather but that was not going to be an option. I could feel my heart beating in my throat I was fighting back the tears and trying to put on a brave face.

Percy fetched a wheelchair, lifted me out of the car and wheeled me to reception.

The receptionist wore glasses, didn't even look up from the book she was reading as I gave her my name and told us to go to the first floor where the nurses would be waiting for me.

As Percy wheeled me down the long passageway with its dull-coloured walls, it felt surreal that this was going to be my new home for a while.

I felt that I did not belong there. It was cold and very clinical. People whizzed around in wheelchairs and did their physio. Some just sat morbidly and stared out into space.

The nurses booked me into a ward. I was engulfed by the black cloud that hung over me and clouded my optimism.

Ushered into my ward, the nurses helped me from my wheelchair into a bed and gave me a laxative. This signalled the beginning of a routine of what my life as a paraplegic would be.

Percy and the kids said their goodbyes and said they would be back in the morning to visit.

I looked at a woman sitting in a wheelchair in a full body cast. She was a pretty blonde woman in her early thirties. She stared out of the window into a solid brick wall, I wondered what answers she was hoping to find on that wall. Her daughter sat on bed next to hers, she was about seven years old and was paralysed. The woman in the bed next to mine had suffered a stroke and wasn't moving at all.

My heart sank. I was not sure what to expect, but this was not it. The setup was dark, eerie, and cold, almost like a movie set for a mental asylum.

The following three days were the worst day of my life since I was shot.

I lay listless in my bed and stared out of my window at the brick wall as there were no nurses to help me turn. I stared out of the window and hoped to find an answer on that dull, red, brick wall just like my roommate did when I arrived.

Later that evening, a nurse brought me dinner and placed it on a trolley behind me. I could smell the food but was unable to move and could not sit upright to pull the tray towards me. The option to ask my new roommates for assistance was definitely out of the question.

I just lay there, doing my best to not think about how hungry I was as I'd only eaten a small slice of toast before leaving Milpark Hospital. This place was a far cry from where I had just come from; warm friendly staff eager to assist here not so much.

I rang the bell for a nurse about six times without any response, so I eventually fell asleep.

I woke up to an awful smell during the early hours of the morning and realised that the laxative the nurse had given me was effective. There were no nurses in sight to assist me to the toilet.

I rang the bell. It was 2 am.

The head nurse eventually marched into the ward at 5 am. She was a large woman greying with a huge mole on her face. She was irritated about me ringing for help and barked at me.

"We are busy bathing quadriplegics and will get back to you later!"

I was left to lay in my own mess for another two hours. The little bit of dignity I had left was gone. I thought to myself, *Well, I will just lie here like a pig in shit.*

I just wanted to die.

If this is what my life was going to be like, I did not want to live that way, I thought.

The nurses eventually arrived. They produced a basin with water that had a thick ring of dirt from previous patients they were bed-bathing and never cleaned or disinfected the basin but rather just filled it with warm water. I proceeded to throw a tempter-tantrum and told them if they came near me with that basin, heads were going to fly.

I wasn't sure how I was going to do this as I couldn't even turn myself, I was really at their mercy. The nurse marched off and came back with a clean basin and mumbled under her breath something about me being a princess. They cleaned me and changed the bedding. Every time they sat me upright, I passed out.

How was I going to finish rehab with my blood pressure being so low?

A really dark feeling of despondency washed over me. I did not want to be here or anywhere. In fact, I wanted out of this madness that was dished up for me.

When Percy arrived that morning, I told him what happened and that I no longer wanted to stay there. He spoke to the management about the way I was mistreated, and they ensured him that it would not happen again.

Later that day, the woman on the bed next to me was released, which left the mother and Daughter sharing the room with me. I came to know their story of why they were there. They were involved in a very tragic car accident when a truck hit them head on when they were on their way back from holiday where the husband and two sons were killed out right and left her and her young daughter paralysed.

I could not help thinking how grateful I was that I was alive and my family was safe. My heart was shattered hearing what this woman had lost. I am not sure how I would have coped with that kind of loss. I was extremely humbled by her story and felt gratitude that my children were spared.

Evenings were really the worst for me. There was only one channel to watch on television, a series called *Carnivàle* that took place during the Great Depression of the 1930s and traced the lives of disparate groups of people in a travelling carnival. It combined a bleak atmosphere with elements of the surreal in portraying struggles between good and evil and between free will and destiny.

I lay watching in the dark with the bed covers pulled right up to my eyes, just enough for me to see what happened. I heard the eerie sound of the wind blowing up the dark long passage and the windows in my room rattling. Moans and weeping emanated in the distance from another ward as the series progressed and became more and more peculiar. I felt unsettled and needed much sleep, so I turned it off. It still haunts me to this day.

The next day, I went to see the management about the food that was fed to us as patients. It was hardly nutritional given a private facility and the amount of training that was happening. Ettien, the friend I made in ICU, was well into his rehab and he was constantly hungry. That afternoon, they brought him a cheese and tomato sandwich hardly enough to fill a strapping young man that was burning a lot of energy while doing physiotherapy.

I heard shouting and a plate smashing on the floor later on, found out he had gone to the kitchen staff to ask for more and they turned him away, then he threw the plate at them. He later told me he was hangry (hungry and angry). By this time, I had informed the management I needed kosher food and could not eat what was there and with that out the way, I started having kosher meals delivered to me. Perhaps, the nurse was right about me being a princess.

I was informed the next afternoon that I would be doing an assessment with a physiotherapist and asked the nurses to put my trainers on for me. They scratched around in my cupboard then told me that I did not have trainers, which I found strange, as I clearly recalled Percy placing them in the side cabinet.

When I called Percy about this, he told me that he had put them with my clothes. I realised that someone stole my trainers and some of my clothes. Percy brought me new trainers and a tracksuit so that I could go for my assessment. At this point, I was very annoyed and wanted to just go home it seemed nothing was going right. What was the point in staying? I was still passing out from very low blood pressure it was dismal situation.

As the nurses moved me to the wheelchair, everything went blank. I woke up on the plinth in the room of the physiotherapist.

She welcomed me back and told me that I has passed out for a while, then opened her file and said, "I am going to do a quick assessment and explain the way forward."

The physiotherapist asked me if I understood what spinal cord injury was and how it was classified according to the part of your spine that was damaged.

The terminology she was using just flew about in my head and didn't make sense to me when she said, "You are classified as a paraplegic and this is your new life. We are here to teach you how to live the new norm."

She took a tissue and told me to close my eyes, then ran the tissue down my chin to my neck and asked me if I could feel it, and I responded with a 'Yes'.

Then she ran the tissue from my chin to just above my breast and asked if I could feel it. I said a little, then she ran the tissue from my shoulder blade to my lower back and asked if I could feel anything. I desperately wanted to answer 'Yes' but I could not feel anything.

I looked at her and told her that she already knew the answer to that question.

She smiled politely and suggested that I should start with aqua therapy.

I told her that I want to go back to my ward. I needed to process all this information that was just given to me. I was in no mood to splash around in a swimming pool. All I wanted was to pick up the phone and talk to my mother but that was no longer an option. Life sucked right now for me and I think she could see it by the look on my face.

She did not argue and smiled again and helped me into a wheelchair, then called a nurse to take me back to my ward.

Then it hit me.

'FUCK! I am paralysed and not just that I'm what they classify me as a T2 paraplegic.'

The physiotherapist's words cut deep into my heart. I felt like I needed to scream so the whole universe could feel my pain but instead I lay on my bed looking on the red brick wall while tears streamed down my face while I searched that wall for clarity and understanding. It was starting to become clear that my situation had a permanence to it. The melancholy words of the therapist engulfed my mind, body and soul.

I was now done with rehab and wanted to leave. I insisted that we found another rehab closer to home.

Three days later, I was booked out and relocated to another rehab centre.

The new rehab centre was closer to home and had a warm, welcoming feeling. I had a room of my own even though there was an open bed next to mine, which made me happy.

The colours in the room were bright and cheerful and my view was an avenue of Jacaranda trees which were in full bloom when I looked out the window, the avenue was this purple archway of trees in full bloom. I felt a peace come over me. This was better than looking onto a red brick wall searching for answers that clearly were not there.

The next day, Elsa, a tall-lanky young lady with a toothy smile that lit up the room was going to be my occupational therapist, she told me that she was going to teach me how to dress myself.

"Yes! Dress myself!"

It took an hour for Elsa to show me what to do and I managed to put on a pair of tracksuit pants and a top, which was a massive challenge for someone like myself who had no core balance.

I flopped around the bed like a jellyfish trying to pull my limp legs through my pants legs and then trying to stay balanced while trying to thread my arms through my shirt, loosing balance and falling over while my body going into uncontrollable spasms. I lay on the bed giggling to myself thinking well '*Lord you do have a sense of humour!*'

Ordinary everyday things that we do each day and took for granted became something that took much more effort and time. Gone were the days of making coffee and carrying it through to the lounge to drink while watching TV. Physically not possible when you must wheel yourself, I can say I did burn myself a few times trying though.

I am not the most patient person so waiting for an elevator because I can't use an escalator was extremely frustrating, but it made me aware of how lazy people are that are able bodies. There were times I would make remarks out loud like "Oh it must be so nice to take the stairs than be in a stuffy elevator."

As each day progressed, I got more skilled at dressing.

The same humdrum routine was repeated each day: eating, dressing and physio in the morning and after lunch. Elsa taught me how to get in and out of the bath and on-and-off the toilet. My body ached from all the exercise but I was not giving up and I knew I was capable of so much more.

In the back of my mind, there was this 1% that maybe they had got it wrong and I will walk again. None of it made sense, it didn't matter how many times they referred to me as a paraplegic. The bullet did not penetrate my spine, there must be a chance I will walk again, I kept telling myself.

When I fell off the toilet, I injured my shoulder blade.

The nurse put on a plaster on the cut on my shoulder. A few days later, I could smell something awful and discovered that it was from the wound. Elsa removed the plaster and found that the wound was badly infected and needed care.

I was faced with constant new challenges and had to maintain a brave face and remain positive but deep down inside, all I wanted was to die.

I wore weird and funny hats in physio to brighten up everyone else's day. Thinking back now, I realise that it was more for me than them, so that I could cope easier.

When I wanted to do more progressed physio like standing up, I was told that I would never be able to walk again, that I was a paraplegic and needed to do the exercises they gave me.

I could not accept that. Surely, they should have encouraged me to at least try.

Late one night, a lady was put in the room with me.

When I asked her what had happened to her, she told me that her husband shot her through the door three times and left her paralysed. She informed me that the police have not found her husband yet and that she was concerned that he would come to the rehab centre and finish her off.

This concerned me. I immediately got scared and felt threatened. All the trauma from my shooting reared its ugly head. I began to feel anxious and jumped at every sound that came from outside.

Even though they had caught the men from the evening, there was still one they had not caught. I was terrified he was coming back for me. When you suffer from PTSD, there are triggers even though you are not sure at the time what they are the anxiety is real to a point where just taking a breath hurts.

I asked Elsa if they could move her to the main ward for her own safety as we were isolated. I felt bad about this, but the last thing I needed was to be in the line of fire if her husband had to come looking for her.

As the days went on, I had the urge to do more physio, but was told that I had to accept my condition. I was not even allowed to do things like standing in a standing frame; this frustrated me. How would I ever know unless I tried? I felt like I was part of a football team but was benched, not ever going to get the nod to participate in the game.

Deep down inside, I felt that I would never know if they did not allow me to try, but they would not listen to me. Deep down there was that 1% what if!

My medical aid funds were almost depleted, and I could not remain at rehab as an in-patient. I had to travel to rehab on a daily basis to complete my physio.

The first day I arrived home after being away from home for nearly a year, it seemed strange yet familiar. Percy got me out of the car onto the wheelchair, my children were so excited that I was finally home. They bounced around me while escorting me into the home where my life was pulled from under me. The dogs came to greet me wagging their tails as if to say, "Finally, our family is complete with Mum home."

We stopped in the entrance hall. What should have been that familiar smell of home, it was masked by the smell of fresh paint and bright colours. I thought how strange that Percy would think a lick of paint would hide or change what happened to us that evening. I felt agitated. Was it because I was back where this nightmare began?

We went to the kitchen, nothing had changed except the colours of the walls. We sat and had a cup of tea together while my children caught me up on all the things going on at school and their lives. It felt longer than a year at this point. I felt like a stranger in my own home being offered tea and treats.

That night, I settled into bed feeling uneasy. This was home but I was not at ease and woke up through the night having flashbacks of that evening. I broke out in a sweat and Percy needed to give me a fresh shirt. He went back to sleep, but I lay watching the silhouette of the tree in the garden fade as the sun rose. That night set the tone for what was to come in the weeks and months ahead.

I knew that being an outpatient was not going to work out.

Percy was reluctant to drive me up and down on a daily basis. We tried for two weeks, but then it became less frequent.

Life got in the way. I had to learn how to adapt the best way I knew how. It is amazing how we take simple things in life for granted like taking a bath or making a cup of tea. This now was no longer as simple as it once was it took planning and even asking for help which I was not accustom too.

One thing I have always been good at is adapting. I have been doing it all my life, why should it be any different? I found ways of making life work the best I could in house that was not adapted for a paraplegic. I soon found solutions to things I had no idea how to do it as not competing rehab, I missed some vital sessions.

For two months, I went for private physio where I focused hard on stabilising my mobility. I stood for 20 minutes at a time between parallel bars and felt positive that I was going to walk again.

Then the rug got ripped from under me.

My physio came to a halt when Percy refused to drive me up to down every day. This did not stop me. I did my physio at home with a walker and was helped by Percy and the kids, but this did not last long either. Percy found excuses not to assist me, saying that he found it too stressful, and the kids were kids.

I did not want to place a burden on my family and just let it go, never to bring it up again. My recruitment business was doing well and gave me a pleasant distraction.

I was back home. The place where the life I had was taken from me.

When I questioned Percy whether the disability fund had paid out because nothing in the house had been adjusted to accommodate my new normality, he was unresponsive. I called the insurance company who confirmed that Percy had requested for payment to be done to his account.

I was shocked and convinced that it was an oversight but when I confronted Percy, he got passive-aggressive and argued that he needed to pay the bills.

I argued that it was my money and that it would make my life easier if I was independent. From the look on Percy's face, it was clear that our conversation was not going to end well.

Percy promised to rectify the matter and make changes in a few months and told me that I had to adjust with what was available.

During the next few weeks, I worked hard in my business and employed someone to assist with sales and admin. Percy just lazed about the house during the day and fetched the kids from school. My workload increased so I asked Percy if he wanted to work as a consultant in my business instead of doing nothing as he was no longer working.

We needed to get our lives on track. I tried desperately to remain positive and motivated so that could rebuild our lives in spite of my physical disposition.

Working hard kept my mind off my new physical status. Simple tasks like bathing and going to the toilet challenged me as new adjustments to the house had not been made and I had to rely on Percy and the kids for assistance.

I lost my independence. It was a reality I had to face and deal with and remained positive that I would be able to cope.

As time lapsed, it was clear that nothing was going to change. All I wanted was for Percy to step up and help me by changing things in the house so that I could regain my independence.

Realising that nothing was going to be done saddened me and made me feel alone although I had the kids and Percy around me.

Percy had to return his dad's car and I found myself working even harder to take care of my family. I knew that the kids needed to get to school and back so bought Percy a second-hand Volvo in cash, feeling relieved to not have any debts.

'Were things improving?' I pondered.

Getting used to a new lifestyle in a wheelchair was more difficult than I thought.

I tried to suppress my constant mental battle by keeping busy, running my business, but the moment I slowed down, depression set in.

My legs could no longer carry me. The freedom I once had was gone.

I could no longer dance with my kids, reach for a glass in the kitchen, bathe myself, and making wild passionate love was definitely not on top of my wish list.

I did not understand how Percy felt about my body now that it was different than before. I even told him that if he wanted to leave me, I would be understanding and would not have any ill feelings towards him. He reassured me that he did not marry me just for body, but for my soulful mind. It was exactly what I needed to hear but did not believe it. In years to come, actions spoke louder than words.

As life wasn't hard enough, when I went to a shopping centre for the first time after the shooting, it was a terrifying experience.

My mother-in-law and myself went to a shopping centre near home to have a coffee and buy some new clothes. Although, I did not have a disability sticker, we got permission to park in a paraplegic parking. The security guard could see I was disabled and was kind enough to let us park.

After an exhausting shopping spree, I got into the passenger seat as Joan put the wheelchair in the boot. I saw a woman marching straight towards me and slam her crutch on the bonnet of the car.

When I asked her what the problem was, she began to shout at me and before I knew what was happening, she had me by the hair and tried to pull me out of the car. I pushed the door further open and knocked her off-balance.

The security guard ran up to us and told the woman to leave me alone as I was disabled. The woman was under the impression that we took advantage of the disabled parking. I found it strange that she was also parked in a disabled parking bay although she was not disabled.

It was the first time I realised how helpless I was. It was one of the many awkward moments and mistreatment to come when I left the house.

With Percy working for me, it placed a lot of unnecessary strain on our marriage, that was not in the best shape. I needed to find him a job and arranged for him to meet with one of my clients. We had coffee with the client and Percy was offered a job.

Little things crept up on me.

As fast as I was making money, it was depleted into secret loans Percy had made with various people when I was hospitalised. He also loaned $160 from a friend, whom he told I would be paying the money back.

What he spent the money on I have no idea to this day. He still hasn't answered for it. I knew that he was in debt with a lot of suppliers that loaned him money when his business went under. Debt collectors arrived at the house the one afternoon looking for Percy and they were looking to give him a beating. I got loud with them, and the one man grabbed me by the hair an told me they would be back and wanted the money. I made a few calls to a friend that let's say you don't want to meet with him in a dark alley. After that phone call, I never heard from these so-called debt collectors.

I could not believe that he abused my disability to renumerate his debts.

Did he really think I would not find out about this?

I should have nipped it in the bud but I let it slide. It did not seem worth the argument.

I had a lot to absorb.

Going from an active person to being restrained in a wheelchair was not an easy task. Simple, menial everyday tasks became problematic. I had to be aware at all times whether or not I was capable of taking on the tasks, or if I might need assistance.

I was injured on so many levels.

I needed someone to take control so that I could recuperate. Catch my breath. Figure everything out.

I lost my mobility, my mother, my marriage, and my independence.

Being disabled is not a life anyone chooses for themselves. There is no way out.

I needed to remain strong for my kids, who needed me more than I needed air, and had to find a way to cope with the constant emotional and physical battle I endured.

Even when I felt at my worst, when I felt that the world closed in on me and that I was dying, I smiled and laughed most of the time.

Deep down inside, I hoped that I would wake up out of the nightmare and realised that nothing was going to change unless I found a way to save myself.

At one stage, there was a glimmer of hope and a buzz word that was on everyone's lips Stem Cells. I was on the internet researching for weeks on end and came across a doctor in Germany that was on the for front of Stem Cells.

I got in contact with him and soon got in touch with someone in South Africa that had had the transfusion done. I made arrangements to meet her but the cost was massive and how was I going to raise this kind of money?

It just happened that this doctor from Germany was going to be in South Africa at the same time I was meant to meet her. I had got a local investigative television show Cart Blanche involved with the story, so they asked if they could come along to meet this doctor and do an interview as this was cutting edge technology for this time in the medical field.

Little did I know that they were doing their own investigation as they were an award winning journalistic investigative programme. The doctor prided himself in the fact he used rabbit Stem Cells in his patients and they recovery was showing positive results. After meeting the patient that had the stem cell treatment and the doctor was interviewed by Carte Blanche.

Just before the show was aired, I got a call from the Carte Blanche producer telling me that this doctor was a fraud, and they were going to expose him. That is where my hope was crushed and I felt myself going on a downward spiral but I still felt that there was always the 1% that was edged into my heart.

Living on medications took the edge off and wine helped to comfort me during the evenings. Bottles of wine flirted shamelessly with me as I emptied them.

It offered an escape from the torment I went through but did not hide my darkest secrets and thoughts.

Yes, I had a broken body, but was my spirit shattered?

Take nothing for granted. Cease every moment to do what you can. And on the occasion you can't, it's okay too. Take a breath and start again. Practice makes perfect.
Tracy Swinson

Chapter 8
Tick-Tick Boom

Just when I thought I had a handle on life and I was in a groove where life seemed to be going well, I had a breather. The handle broke!

Seven years into my new life, when I was settled and had adapted to the best of my abilities, I decided one early Sunday morning to have a lovely hot bubble bath. This was strange for me as I loved my showers but for no reason, I just wanted to have a lovely soak in a hot bath. Percy and my daughter Nicole helped me into the bath.

I settled in deep thought, my mind drifting to so many things, yet nothing. I lathered my body gently. When I ran my soapy hands over my breasts, then froze and then slowly ran my hands over my right breast again, I sat upright when I felt a lump the size of an egg. My heart pounded as the blood ran from my face my worst nightmare had reared its ugly head.

How could I have missed it? I thought as my stomach churned. Deep down inside, I knew what it was, as it was the same lump my mother had. I had been vigilant by going annually for mammograms, how could this be?

When Percy helped me out of the bath, I looked at him with tears in my eyes and told him that I found a lump in my breast.

He inspected my breast and assured me rolled his eyes.

"It could be nothing. Just get it checked out," he said.

The rest of the day, I was quiet, sick to the pit of my stomach. I lay awake the whole night, my thoughts darting back and forth.

The next morning, I sat anxiously at the radiologist and waited for my mammogram and sonar. A million thoughts raced through my mind. Deep down inside, I knew I had a battle coming.

The radiologist told me that it seemed like a blocked milk duct after the mammogram was done, but when they did a sonar and he brought in another doctor for a second opinion, a tear ran down my face. I wiped it away and told myself to get a grip. I knew that another battle lay ahead.

I was referred to Dr Benn, one of South Africa's most prominent breast cancer specialists, who sent me for a biopsy to confirm what I already knew.

Nicole stood bravely beside me during the biopsy and held my hand. When she looked at what they were doing, she turned her head away and went pale in the face and had to sit down. I was relieved that I could not see what the doctor was doing during the procedure. I smiled at Nicole trying to put her mind at ease, but I felt like I was going to implode with fear.

When the day of the results arrived, Percy, Nicole and I sat in Dr Benn's office, which looked more like a homely lounge.

Dr Benn made small talk, then looked directly at me and said, "The results are positive. You have breast cancer."

I heard nothing after that. I was sitting trying to imagine how my mum felt when those same words were delivered to her.

When I snapped out of my disbelief, she asked me if I wanted to remove one or both my breasts.

I decided on both being removed. It was a no brainer that the feminine mounds on my chest were ticking time bombs. You get what I mean: "Tick-tick boom, dead."

Dr Benn scheduled a double mastectomy for two days later.

That morning, I was in high spirits. I knew half the battle was won by having my breasts removed.

Ten…nine…eight…seven…And then they were gone.

I woke up in an ICU ward where there was eight other women and looked down at my chest where my breasts once were. I was now as flat as an ironing board and let out a loud giggle.

I heard someone crying from across the room, and another person sniffing next to me while I sat with a smile on my face. Call me crazy but it just didn't make sense to cry over something that could take your life.

When the nurse came to check on me, I asked her why these women were crying, and she told me that they were weeping because their breasts had been removed.

"Are they insane?" I laughed loudly. "Those things can kill you. They killed my mother!"

The nurse hushed me. I think she felt that I was being rather insensitive.

Within a couple of hours, I was moved to private room, away from the weeping women.

I thought it strange that someone would mourn something that could potentially kill them.

A lot of us don't understand the stages of mourning, me included. I always manage to sweep it under the rug and think that I will deal with it later. Dr Benn did try arranging counselling for me but I told them I was fine. This is what I found out later about the stages of mourning.

There are seven stages: shock, denial, anger, bargaining, depression, testing and acceptance. I think I just skipped to acceptance which I can tell you from my experience later in life, it is not healthy. It is important to go through these stages so you can heal better and not have to revisit those emotions at a later stage.

Mastectomy is a pretty word for amputation now if they had said that it may have had a different effect on me. It is amazing how a simple word can change a perception and an emotion.

The following day, I was visited by Dr Slabbert, a pleasant looking plastic surgeon with gentle eyes and a sexy voice, who explained to me how they were going to proceed with the reconstruction surgery. He explained they put incisors under my skin to expand the skin, that would allow for the implants. He also told me about the reconstructing of my nipples.

It was a lot to absorb.

The surgery would only happen after chemotherapy. Not only did I lose my breasts, I had to allow them to inject chemicals into my veins that would basically destroy everything in my body to kill the cancer cells.

I did research as to what foods would be best to support my body during and after chemo and I would need to change my bad eating habits. It seemed like a fool-proof plan going forward but little did I know what was to come. Surviving chemotherapy was going to be brutal and what you put in your body didn't matter. It was more what you could keep down; I ended up eating salt and vinegar crisps, cream soda and gingersnap biscuits.

When I arrived home four days later, I never stopped to conceive what I had been put through. I was completely naïve about what was to happen next.

Before I knew it, Percy, Nicole and I sat in a crowded waiting room with wall-to-wall cancer patients.

I tried not to make eye contact with those that sat around me. The desperation and defeat on their face troubled me. They sat waiting for their next treatment and hoped that it was the one that would save their lives.

I had no idea what to expect as I sat quietly and waited for the oncologist to discuss my chemo treatment. The only thing I expected was that my beautiful long hair would be gone soon. I wanted to get up and run but that was not an option.

When we settled down in Dr G's office, she was a short plum Greek lady with gentle eyes and spoke in a compassionate way, she talked us through the chemo treatment and what to expect.

I saw her mouth moving but absorbed nothing. It was all surreal to me. I felt like a lamb being led to slaughter. There was no running away from it.

"How hard could this actually be?" I questioned. A drip would be inserted into my vein and chemicals would flow through my veins. It would kill my entire immune system.

I was in high spirits the following week after I had a blood test done and was on the list for my treatment.

I chose not to be in the waiting room full of cancer patients. I needed my head to be in a positive state. I told the receptionist that we would be waiting in the coffee shop and to call me when treatment was ready.

Reminding myself that I was a statistic, I needed to be in a healthy mental state with positive thoughts, listening to soothing music to calm my soul and mentally prepared myself with positive affirmations.

Percy was occupied on his phone when I was called for treatment.

I arrived in the treatment room with a huge smile plastered on my face and gave the nurse a high-five.

"Let's do this."

Little did anyone know how terrified I was given my mother died and my daughter may be at risk as she may have the defective gene, which Dr Benn pointed out.

Patients around me weren't that enthusiastic and not sure what to make of the crazy woman in the wheelchair, who was breathless and hyped up to tackle her chemo.

What they did not know was that I was terrified and needed to remain in a positive space, otherwise it would have gone downhill fast.

I saw the same familiar faces each time I went for chemo, they just sat there, waiting. I noticed that some of the regular faces were no longer there, and I wondered what had happened to them. I tried to convince myself they were fine and pulled through their treatment but not all of it was true.

They were going through the same routine and had given up. It saddened me.

It was not long before I started losing my hair and began to feel the effect of chemo to the extent that I was hospitalised with a superbug that could only be treated intravenously.

I spent ten days in hospital, hooked to a drip.

The woman next to me was fighting pancreatic cancer and was extremely cheerful when her family visited her. One evening, her family were visiting and her grandchild asked her if he could play something for her on the violin, he played amazing grace. It was such a beautiful piece of music and brought tears to my eyes.

Early hours that morning, I heard a crashing noise I called out to her she did not answer me. I rang for the nurses and they came in and found her on the bathroom floor. She had collapsed, they helped her into bed; by the morning, she had passed away.

I was fortunate to experience the close bond of family and how they stuck together until the bitter end. Experiencing this made me realise how fragile life really is.

It made me think about my own family. My relationship with Percy was not great, he remained extremely aloof and was often missing in action.

I realised that it was not something I should focus on, but rather on my healing and getting through chemo.

One morning, while waiting for breakfast, a man wondered into my ward and started a conversation with me after chatting with him, I asked him what had brought him here. He told me about his brush with cancer twice and how he beat it. This is exactly what I needed to hear, a success story.

I will always remember Raymond's story and we have remained Facebook friends ever since. He didn't realise at the time what an impact his story had on my state of mind. Raymond has done a lot of cancer awareness for the Sunflower Fund where he has climbed all the highest mountains and peaks around the world, the one particular climb he did was called Vinson Massif in 2013 where he planted a flag with all the cancer survivors faces on it with a quote including mine.

Vinson Massif is the highest mountain of Antarctica, lying in the Sentinel Range of the Ellsworth Mountains, which stand above the Ronne Ice Shelf near the base of the Antarctic Peninsula. The massif is located about 1,200 kilometres (750 mi) from the South Pole and is about 21 km (13 mi) long and 13 km (8.1 mi) wide. At 4,892 metres (16,050 ft), the highest point is Mount Vinson, which was named in 2006 after Carl Vinson, long-time member of the U.S. Congress from the state of Georgia.

Vinson Massif was first seen in 1958 and first climbed in 1966. An expedition in 2001 was the first to climb via the Eastern route, and took GPS measurements of the height of the peak. As of February 2010, 700 climbers have attempted to reach the top of Mount Vinson.

I was released from hospital the next day.

The phone rang off the hook the next morning. I'd been released from hospital and was too weak to get out of bed. Percy answered and informed me that the hospital received the results of my CT scan. My life was in danger.

I had pulmonary embolisms, a blood clot blocked and stopped blood flow to an artery in my lung and I needed to urgently return to the hospital. I refused to go back to hospital. I had enough, so Percy arranged with them to give him the medication.

They gave Percy injections to give me that would dissolve the blood clots and I was put on warfarin, a prescription medication used to prevent harmful blood clots from forming or growing larger.

This was now going to be for life. One treatment followed the other, my body was taking a beating; I could not keep food down and I was sore and exhausted, feeling nausea all the time.

My business had come to a complete halt as I was too weak to run it. One of my friends was out of work and offered to help me. The trusting person I am, I gave her full access to my business and clients after bringing her up to speed. I felt like this was going to be the answer to me being able to focus on getting better and not worrying about my business.

Fortunately, a policy paid out and I could sustain paying bills and my medical aid which allowed me to continue my treatment.

Little did I know that Percy's business was in failing dismally and he had not told me about his situation. He asked me to assist him as he had not paid rent on a shop that the landlord had locked him out, I agreed to loan him the money and told him that it needed to be returned before the next debit order of the medical aid came through. He assured me that it would be settled, and I gave him the money so that he could resume is business.

The next month my medical aid bounced, and I could not go for my next treatment.

A huge argument erupted between Percy and me. I discovered that he'd been lying about his business and that it was failing to the point of no return. I now was put in a predicament that I could not continue my treatment and how was this going to impact me later down the line. I was so angry with Percy, I had no-one to turn to and ask for assistance.

I remained home unable to complete my chemo treatment.

It wasn't long before Percy's business folded, and he was jobless again.

I also found out that my friend had stolen my business from me, she told clients that I was severely ill and that I would not survive and transferred my clients into her agency.

There I was. I had not completed chemo treatment, and Percy was unemployed and had no business to go back to.

Matters were dismal, we were completely broke and had to sell items in the house and jewellery to put food on the table. Our car was repossessed as Percy had not made payments and he kept reassuring me that everything was fine.

I was oblivious to how dire our situation was. It broke my heart to know that my kids were put through this.

My kids and I were watching television one night when the bank repossessed our car.

Nicole answered the door. I sat there, wrapped in a blanket with my bald head, recovering from the aftereffects of chemo, trying desperately to not think about the fact that I had no breasts.

My heart sunk when the Sherriff told me that they had to take the car. I negotiated with the sheriff as I knew I had a client that was about to pay me so when I received payment, I brought the payments up to-date.

Percy just stood there.

My kids had no choice but to cope with the situation there was no hiding the fact that we were broke. This is a lot for my children to experience on top to the shooting and me getting breast cancer, I felt hopeless. '*Did I fail them as a mother?*' I wondered.

Although my body was in pain, I got up the next morning and went to my office to start my business from scratch. I phoned all my clients and managed to rekindle two clients by the end of the week. I sat with a blanket draped over my shoulders and resting my head in my hands by the end of the day the effects of chemo still made my body ache.

I pushed on every day with a smile on my face and pretended that everything was fine, which it wasn't. I felt like I had to take the lead as head of the family as weak as I was.

Percy became a couch potato, sitting around, doing less than nothing to go out and find a job, or look for any open positions.

I felt this cycle was on repeat and it was.

I had to take action and called the company I first got him a job with and asked if they had any positions open, which they did, so I asked Percy to meet up with them and get his job back. Percy was back at work, and I felt like things were going to get better three months into Percy being back at work earning a great salary. The sheriff arrived the one evening while I was making dinner.

I answered the door, and he said that Percy had not made any further payments on the car. I was confused this must be some mistake he was working why would he not make the payments. This time there was no negotiating they took the car when I looked over my shoulder towards the door, I saw my children standing there with Percy in the background. I was so angry and disappointed in him, *what man does this…* I thought to myself.

Thank goodness I had stashed money away when my business was picking up again but now, I had to take the last of my live savings to buy Percy another car. I was yet to get myself one, but it was essential for the kids to get to school and back.

When I look back now, Nicole reminded me of how awful it was when I was hospitalised. The electricity was cut due to non-payment, and she had to study for her matric exams by candlelight. She kept all of this to herself until years later because she did not want to worry me more than I already was. She always went out of her way to protect me and shield me from further disappointment and guard her younger brother from the awful truth and harsh reality of our lives.

This was a lot for a young teenager to take on her shoulders and a lot of unnecessary pressure at her young age of seventeen years old. She essentially took on the role of a mother when I was ill; cooking, cleaning, and taking care of me, while she still had to maintain good grade to pass high school.

I had to go back to the oncologist for a check-up every three months. She was concerned that I had not finished my treatment and told me that she needed to keep a close eye on me. I felt as the months rolled by, I was constantly looking over my shoulder was because I did not complete my treatment going to come back and bite me. I could still smell the chemo coming out of my pores and yet I had not even finished my treatment.

The day of my reconstruction surgery arrived, and I was looking forward to it. There is something to be said that no matter what anyone says otherwise for me not having breasts, I did not feel feminine at all, and the scars made it that much harder for me to look at myself and love the person looking back at me in the mirror.

I once again laid back in the operating theatre and counted backwards and awoke to two wonderful new mounds on my chest again.

I felt feminine again and happy that the ordeal was now behind me. It was really hard because I had to use my arms to help me transfer and push my wheelchair, so recovery took longer than usual.

Unfortunately, there were more obstacles to overcome. I needed to redo my breast reconstruction.

I was transferring one evening from my chair to the bed and noticed my shirt was covered in blood and called Nicole and Percy for assistance. Nicole went pale when she removed my bloody shirt. I could tell by the look on her face that this was serious. I laughed about it and told them it would be like changing a tyre.

At the breast clinic, the nurses discovered that my stiches had torn open and that my implant and rib cage was visible. My doctor was out of town and the nurses had to patch me up.

Round two. My implants were replaced the following day like I said changing a tyre.

While I was in my ward recovering, the phone rang it was Constable Dube from the police station informing me that the 5th man from the night of my shooting had just been arrested, almost 10 years to the day.

I always wondered what happened if they ever caught him and finally, I had my answer. I thought I had put it to bed years ago but hearing this good news, I let out a sigh of relief and realised that this chapter was really closed and over.

I was finally on the mend until two years later when I fell out of the car while I transferred from my wheelchair. Luckily, I used my left arm to break the fall.

A few weeks later, I did not feel well and was tired all the time it felt like flu symptoms but never developed more than that. I decided to go see my doctor whom suggested going for a sonar only to find out I had a burst implant third time.

Lucky, I thought.

Here we go again. Back to surgery. This time, it felt like I changed a tyre and upgraded from Dunlop to Pirelli's. I needed something more durable as I used my arms a lot. There was a lot of back and forth between Dr Joe and I as I wanted bigger implants, and he would not budge but did agree to go with high profile implants.

This was the last and final reconstruction surgery, and I was pleased with the outcome. The scaring is so minimal that you would have to be up close to see it and the nipples look real even though they are made from two circular pieces of skin from my stomach. Dr Jo was a genius.

One would think that with a double mastectomy and reconstruction surgery with chemo all would be well, but there are many variants and side effects.

I went for a check-up after I completed my treatment. When they did a CT scan, they discovered black marks on my lungs and I was immediately ordered to do a CT guided biopsy which generally resulted in fewer complications, a faster recovery time, and avoidance of general anaesthesia.

I was terrified as they laid me down on my stomach and with the help of the CT scanner, they made an incision between my ribcage and fed a tube into my lung. They instructed me to take a deep breath and as I did, they injected a blue powder into my lung. As I released my breath the blue powder exited my mouth. When they pulled the tube from my lung, it collapsed. They rushed me into the theatre where I was put onto a breathing apparatus while the doctors did a biopsy on my lung.

When I awoke in ICU, it once again felt like a bus had parked on my chest.

A few days later, my oncologist told me that I was diagnosed with sarcoidosis, a side-effect from chemo, in which there is an abnormal collection of inflammatory cells that form clumps in the lungs, skin or lymph nodes. My body's antibodies fought itself which caused my lungs to form crystals. The treatment suggested for this was small doses of chemo tablets.

I refused further treatment and decided to only do a check-up once a year. Up to now, I have been fine.

I thought a lot about my mum and what she must have gone through when she was doing her chemo treatment and did not have anyone to discuss the details with her. Although we talked, I never fully understood how she felt when she'd lost her breast.

Like myself, I kept a smile on my face and never really told my kids how I really was feeling, and I guess she did the same trying to protect me from the reality of cancer and the effect it has on one's phycological mind.

Writing this today, I can confirm that hearing about breast cancer and experiencing it is much harder than anyone can ever imagine.

Worldwide, women who have breast cancer go through the same process of reluctant shock and eventual acceptance. I was fortunate to have my family by my side and cannot begin to imagine what it would have been like if there was no-one to cheer me along and share my tears.

Breast cancer can be beaten if it is discovered early. When I think about how big my lump was, and how I never noticed it, I thank God that I took a bath that morning and not a shower because it would have gone by undetected and could have resulted in me losing my life to breast cancer like my mother.

It is much more difficult to find when you are taking a shower. I urge woman to do regular self-exams that takes two minutes and what to look out for. Going through this experience I felt I needed to give back and have done by doing corporate talks about breast cancer and my fight. My story was featured in *Destiny Businesswoman* magazine.

I grew stronger and stronger and was soon back in full swing at work.

The loss I had experienced was a daily reminder when I looked at the scars across my new breasts.

I became conscious of this and confident within myself and never revealed how I felt. The loss broke my heart even when I was smiling and making jokes, that was to hide my fear and pain I was feeling. I large part of me felt guilty my family had been through so much I did not want to burden them with my deep feelings of pain, so I masked it with a smile and buried it deep in my soul. I could not dwell on it and needed to look ahead and take control of my life.

I was aware that Percy saw me differently, more so now than when I lost my ability to walk. He became distant and I knew that our marriage was over. He became more reluctant when I suggested that we should consider marriage counselling and eventually agreed to go, but after two sessions it was history. I don't know at what point he stopped loving me but he did and nothing I did or tried to change that fact, it remained.

One day, when we arranged to meet my dad for lunch, I cut myself and Percy fetched his first aid kit from the car. He sat down on the bed next to me and when he opened the first aid kit, condoms fell out. I saw his reaction and when I questioned him about having condoms in his first aid kit, he blamed my son, Kyle.

When I asked Kyle about the condoms, he laughed at me and asked why he would keep condoms in a car he had no access to.

My heart sank.

I tried to sit Percy down and discuss the condoms he denied that they were his and turned passive-aggressive when I pushed him for the truth. The truth was right in front of me, but I needed to hear it from his mouth, and he was not ever going to admit it.

I was exhausted from a year of chemo and numerous reconstructions. I felt like I had just got off a battlefield much like my pops described. After everything I had endured that year and decided to let it slide, I needed to catch my breath and collect myself before I fell apart. I felt that I started to shut myself off emotionally and physically from Percy what we had felt tainted.

This was not what I signed up for. Or was it?

Letting go of what could potentially kill you takes courage!
Tracy Knight

Chapter 9
Crazy Not Crazy

I was out of rehab about 18 months after being shot and I thought I was coping well in spite of the unfortunate hand I was dealt.

I felt anxious and on edge and could not figure out why. As I did not want Percy and the kids to go through anymore reminders of what *that night* had done to me, I kept quiet and bottled my feelings.

During the next six months, my uneasiness grew worse. I would jump out of my skin whenever loud noises erupted around me and panicked when the bedroom door shut closed. Even with the lick of paint on the walls of our home, the memories of that evening echoed through the passage where I lay after the bullet slammed into my chest and paralysing me instantly.

My nightmares started. I woke up in cold sweat after I'd relive the occurrences of that evening when I was shot during our home invasion.

'What if's' surfaced in my dreams, triggers that were set off by the traumatic events. The same reoccurring dream where I was trying to run but my feet would not move and then a loud gun shot. That would shake me from my nightmare and I would lie there the rest of the night afraid to close my eyes because I would be having the same dream over like it was on loop.

It was exhausting. In the back of my mind, there was the one perpetrator they had not caught, and I was so scared he was coming back to finish the job I know it really doesn't make sense but when you this exhausted your thoughts are often muddled.

It was impossible for me to focus. I was exhausted and everyone around me irritated me. Thoughts of suicide flashed through my mind. I wanted to end it all and could no longer live with the fear in my heart. It was as if I was forced to watch a horror movie and could not find the remote to switch it off.

Depression is a lonely person's disease.

I never really knew what this meant but can now affirm that people will never be able to see what's going on in your head and ever understand the anguish that anchors you unless they have gone through similar experiences themselves.

Unless you have experienced trauma, you will never understand it. You might function to the best of your abilities but cannot surface from the despair you feel.

There is a heavy burden that suffocates you. Even the soft rays of the sunlight felt heavy on my skin and forced me to crawl back under the duvet with the hope that the feeling of gloom will pass. It doesn't though; you wake up with the same heavy feeling and no matter how hard you try to shake it you can't. How can you even explain something to someone that you yourself don't understand?

It's hard to battle something that is invisible. Something you do not understand.

I kept thinking about mousy Lizl who was clinically depressed and visited me in the ICU after she'd read my story in the newspaper and considered ending her life. My story gave her hope. If I could have understood her state of mind, it would have helped her. I never understood what she was trapped in, her desperation, I'd never been depressed or felt what she told me.

I thank God that despite my severely medicated state and that I could not grasp her emotional state of mind, I managed to comfort her and inspire her with my story not giving up the will to fight. Little mercies like this saved Lizl's life. I wish I could see her again and tell her that I now have a full understanding of what she went through.

Percy observed my decline and wisely placed all medication and sharp objects out of my reach. The only medication I had access to was the ones he administered to me when I needed.

I was desperate to not relive that night again and lay awake with thoughts of what was wrong with me, of my beautiful kids who loved me as I was and that I would never abandon them.

I visited my GP to see what could be done to prevent this feeling of helplessness and escape the abyss that engulfed me.

Dr W was a young doctor and up-to-date with all the latest narcotics that were peddled by pharmaceutical reps and I had hope that this was going to be the answer. The doctor told me that I was in a state of depression and post-traumatic stress disorder (PTSD), a mental health condition that's triggered by a terrifying event. He put me on a cocktail of anti-depressants, sleeping pills and medication for the nerve pain.

It was just what I needed. I felt light again, the nightmares dissolved and I could function normally, be emotionally available for my kids.

It was great to not have any worries and get a good night's rest. For a while, things were normal and I enjoyed spending time with my kids and entertained their friends. As a parent, you do the best you can for your children. We don't always get it right. I wish each child came with a manual.

Funny story—One January it was back to school and I had enrolled my oldest Kyle into a private school. He was excited to be starting school and so was I so much so I pulled up to the school, hugged and kissed him good luck and told him I would fetch him after school. I just arrived at work and received a call from his school, the receptionist told me that I had dropped my son off a week early.

I apologised and felt so embarrassed. I can't imagine what they must have thought about me. Kyle was traumatised by this; he never lets me live it down. Thinking back now, I never noticed when dropping him off that there were no other cars in sight or children. I honestly can't remember if there were other parents and children being dropped off.

We can laugh about it now but back then, I felt terrible and I had failed as a mother. When I tell this story today, I can barely get through it without laughing hysterically.

I felt invincible. Human. That I was part of the world again.

A year passed.

I woke up during the early hours of the morning and when I felt slightly anxious, I increased the dosage of my sleeping pills and anti-depressants. This was effective for a while, but soon my body adjusted, and I had to increase my dosage again to not feel depressed. Before long, I was hooked on two-and-a-half sleeping tablets, opioids and two anti-depressants, with the additional addiction of downing two bottles of wine per night.

I was unaware that I had become an addict.

It served me well for a while and soon, I drifted out of the present and became a zombie that took each day as it came.

Numb inside, I detached from my emotions.

'What was happening to me? Why could I not shake off the depression?'

At night, I stared at the tick-tock of the clock. The only way I could escape this was by taking more sleeping pills. I fell into bed and would do stupid things, I would take my tablets and not go to bed and then try stand up and go make tea and have constant fights with my son Kyle for no reason.

I created havoc.

My youngest son Greigan was convinced that I could walk so when I asked him to bring me my walker, he would not question it. Nicole caught him and took the walker away from him. This happened on a regular basis, and he would argue with his siblings.

I was self-medicating and drank wine every night to knock me out. My children told me things I'd done the night before. I could not remember anything and told them that they were lying, they all had my dark sense of humour.

After closing a deal with a prospective client one morning, I looked up from my desk and could not recall a word from our conversation. I was completely blank and felt sick to the pit of my stomach. I did sustain short-term memory damage from the car accident with Megan but this was something else, this was far more sinister.

Was I losing my mind? I questioned as I thought about my Gran who had dementia and got scared. Google-searched to check whether dementia was inherited or not, I found that it was not. I then Googled the medication that I had been taking and found that memory loss was one of the symptoms.

Doctors will always tell you not to self-diagnose or research symptoms on Google—me rolling my eyes! Google was my friend then and it guided me to the next part of my journey. Now that I knew I had not inherited dementia, it had to be something else.

A panic gripped me when I realised that my kids were truthful and did not spin lies.

'How will I be able to live without medication?' I asked myself.

After taking sleeping tablets, my behaviour escalated into chaos. No-one knew what would happen after 8 pm, whether I would injure myself because I forgot that I could no longer walk.

Conflicted, I knew that I could not live like that that any longer and had no idea how I would cope if I stopped.

I was terrified.

When I visited new GP in the morning, a very gentle old grey-haired man, I told him my story: from the tragic shooting to my post-traumatic stress disorder, the medication I was on and my memory loss. He told me that the medication was meant for a short period only and that I had developed a dependency on pills and alcohol.

What? Not me! I thought to myself. I have always been in control. He was mistaken.

As he spoke, I realised that the person he was describing was me and it felt like someone told me that I was dying.

'*How did this happen? Where did the time go this last five years?*'

I was in a total mess.

He suggested that I should consider rehab, but I did not want that stigma attached to my character and asked him politely to assist me in coming off what I was on at home.

I did not want to spend any more time away from my kids like I'd done when I was shot. It took some time to convince the doctor that I would be able to do it on my own, but he eventually agreed.

I started with a new prescription for less intrusive medication and put my mind to it that I would be able to take control. I know myself. When I decide to do something, nothing will change my determination to reach my goal.

I coped well the first couple of days. I thought that it was not too bad, not sure what the doctor was thinking when he suggested rehab.

As the days ticked by, I became more restless, ill-tempered and was cranky the whole time. I got phantom itching and scratched a hole on the tip of my nose, I got hot and cold shivers and terrible headaches. My thoughts became incredibly scrambled, I felt out of control and snapped at everyone, turning their lives into hell the next three months. My children told me that it was like living with a meth monster.

I sweated profusely at night and my nightmares returned, thinking that I would never make it, but deep down inside of me there was a little voice that told me that I would be able to do it. If I survived a bullet and cheated death, then nothing was impossible.

The little voice was my only support and before long, I beat my drug and alcohol addiction. Yes, addiction! People whose lives were not in order could easily lose control and become substance dependant.

I think that going through this, if I had to do it again, I would definitely opt for rehab. This is something I do not want to relive and today, I am so careful and mindful of the medications I take.

I reminded myself every day of how I'd lost control and kept myself in check.

There were good days and bad days. I reminded myself on stormy days that there was nothing wrong with feeling down in the dumps, and that I would appreciate sunnier days when they surfaced.

I learnt that anti-depressants were necessary but that it was not natural to always feel euphoric and be on a constant high. It was okay to have down days as long as you could ensure that it did not last for too long, have regular check-ups and a clear understanding of what medication you are on. We too often trust doctors when getting prescription medication and not understanding the side effects properly.

I believe that without bad days, you cannot truly appreciate good days and should always maintain a balance.

Some of us need more than medication. We need someone to talk to that will motivate and support us, help us cope with our mental disease, trauma, and our emotions.

Life was great then suddenly I am faced with a life altering news I had breast cancer. The fight was real and even though I came out victorious, that familiar dark feeling engulfed me once again. Here I was again, that familiar feeling of darkness and no zest for life, it had become all too much for my soul to deal with. There is only so much one person can endure before the bow breaks but in my case, I was shattered into a million little pieces.

In 2017, I sat alone in my room holding Percy's unregistered pistol and tried desperately to load the magazine. My hands shook as I held this heavy piece of metal that was going to aid me to putting an end to the broken sadness I could not shake, although I was calm inside.

I decided that I could no longer go on and wanted to end my misery. Remember, I said earlier in my book that guns are not dangerous but the person holding the gun. I was no better than the man that shot me. I was about to do the very same thing but to myself.

The loss in my life was overwhelming: I lost the use of my legs. I lost my mother to breast cancer, and I lost my own breasts to cancer. The straw that broke the camel's back was when Percy also told me that he wanted to leave me. When he told me that he wanted to leave, I felt like a toy a child has broken and tossed away in a corner, never to be played with again.

I guess it stems from when my dad left when I was born and me being kicked out of home. These losses were also triggered later in life. I could not deal with anymore loss in my life. I'm sure I could have dealt with the losses if I had been given more time to grieve but I always kept up a brave face and made jokes, telling myself to never look back.

It caught up with me even though I never knew that this was the case.

My hands trembled as I held the loaded pistol in my hand. I remember that it was a hot day. I closed the bedroom door, leaving the dogs on the other side, I was resolute in my decision to end my life. I felt euphoric. It was like nothing I had ever felt before.

It's strange that when you make a choice like that, it feels as if the world has been lifted from your shoulders. There were no more burdens to carry. You could breathe freely and let out a sigh of relief.

Just then my housekeeper/caregiver, Elizabeth, walked into the room with the laundry that had just be pressed, she put the clothing on the bed.

I could see the concern in her eyes as they glistened with tears, then gently took the gun from my hand, asking me, "What are you doing?"

I was not expecting her to walk in on me and my heart sank when she took the pistol from me. That euphoric feeling dissipated and I felt hopeless. I felt like my soul was shattered into a million pieces.

Had she been a few minutes late, I would not be here telling my story.

She never left my side as she reached for her mobile and called Percy but he did not answer, then called Percy's mum, who immediately made her way to our home to take me to my GP. We sat with the GP until she could get hold of a psychologist.

From the time I had a gun in my hand to sitting in front of the GP, I felt like I was suspended in time.

I was in a daze. All I could think of was not wanting to live.

'What was the point of living with this feeling of helplessness?'

'This was my life, surely I had the right to decide if I wanted to live or die!'

The psychologist was nerdy, she has long curly hair that was tied back, she wore glasses and no make-up, and wore an over-stretched jersey and denims.

Her first question was what brought me to this point in my life?

I could not and did not want to talk. It was too painful. I had no idea how it got to this point and tearfully stared out of the window.

Where do I start? I thought. *I don't even know who I am right now.*

I did not recognise the broken woman who sat in the wheelchair and stared blankly out of the window. I used to be a bright and happy outgoing person, now I did not want to be around the stranger I had become.

I told the psychologist how I broken I felt and that I could not go on. I wanted to end this misery of a life I was living.

After a long discussion, the psychologist wanted to commit me to a psych ward, but I would not hear of it. Determined to go home and finish off what I started, I was very convincing, but she saw through it. After hours of chatting and negotiating, she convinced me to go to the psych ward. They tried to get hold of Percy to tell him what had happened, but he had turned off his phone and was having coffee with the woman he worked with.

I thought it was a joke when I was booked into the psych ward. I felt fine, there was nothing wrong with me. My mind was clear, I didn't want to be there anymore. It is strange how the highs and lows come that you think there is nothing wrong you suddenly feel fine.

Life was looking up when I met the psychiatrist who came to see me. He was really cute with long blonde hair, blue eyes, and the cutest smile—he had the whole surfer look going for him.

Maybe this was a wave I could surf.

When he was ready to take notes and asked me what had happened, I laughed and told him that he needed more paper.

Without blinking an eyelid, he scribbled away taking notes in a typical doctors eligible hand writing, as I spoke in a monotone voice. It was like a stuck record, me retelling my story over and over as if it was going to change the ending I foresaw in my mind.

Percy at this point got up and left the room mumbling under his breath, "I can't hear this shit again." Perhaps, he was right it was like a story on loop even I was tired of it that's why I wanted out. If my own husband had had enough, imagine the relief I felt when I wanted to end this journey.

After twenty minutes, he called a nurse for more paper and looked up at me with his blonde hair hanging in his tanned face and gave a gentle smile.

"You could be a case study," he said. Standing with a stack of paper where he had made notes on my life and most intimate thoughts.

Wow! All I could think about was how to get out of there, nothing he said sank in with me.

I took the medication he prescribed and got a good night's sleep.

That little voice inside me stirred during the early hours of the morning. I was trapped in a psych ward and was having a conversation with myself. I convinced myself that my life held meaning and purpose and that I should persevere and push forward or else I would be there for a long time. That thought terrified me. By 8 am the next morning, I was dressed and even made my own bed.

I was ready to leave. I had practised in my head what I was going to say to convince 'surfer doctor' that I was fine and wanted to go home. Like I mentioned before, when I make up my mind, there is nothing that will deter me. I had a whole speech prepared and had a compelling argument as to why I did not belong in the psych ward.

When the psychiatrist walked into my ward wearing his baggies and a surf T-shirt, with his hair tied in a manbun, it was a very chilled look for a Saturday morning.

He was on time at 11am, he talked but I did not hear a word he was saying. I just saw his mouth moving. When it stopped moving, I told him that I was, and will be going home. It was important for me to fix my problems at home, and not hide in the psych ward.

He did not buy any of it and reminded me that I wanted to take my own life.

After much back-and-forth deliberation, we reached an understanding. I admitted that I was broken and needed help and would remain an outpatient if he'd release me. I would see him twice a week and remain loaded on psych meds.

Little did I know that I was on suicide watch at home, every move I made was monitored. With the help of medication, I was easy to control.

I was like a happy zombie just going about my day-to-day duties, numb to any feelings that once tortured me. One day rolled into the next, I had no sense of time but it was a small price to pay to feel no darkness but I knew I was broken I could feel my soul rattle around at night when I tried to sleep.

I questioned my state of mind and asked what I had learnt from my past experience, realising that my medication only treated the symptoms. I needed to get to the bottom of why I was not able to get a grip on life.

A bipolar friend of mine who was no stranger to depression suggested that I saw her psychiatrist and booked an appointment.

When I sat in Dr Marco's reception, I looked at graffiti his patients had written on the walls. There were some very quirky and sombre scribblings mostly in thanks to the doctor.

'*Was I mad?*' I questioned. '*What was wrong with me and how did I end up where I was?*'

Emotions are strange. We don't always know where to place or how to deal with them. They are overpowering and can easily consume one's whole life.

Before I could finish my thoughts pondering my life, I went into Dr Marco's office.

His gentle face and eyes looked at me from behind his glasses, he had a salt-and-pepper look and wore a checker shirt. He seemed slightly scattered at first but then settled down and gave me his full attention, not bothering with notes, and just listened.

Here we go again, I thought to myself and anticipated him asking me what brought me there, with me then reciting my story.

Instead, he asked, "Tell me how your day is going so far."

I did not know whether to be angry, cry or laugh. At $200 for the session, he wanted to know how my day went. I played along and proceeded to tell him that I was doing alright. That I needed help, other than medication, to get me through the day, let alone the life I was living. We never spoke about anything in particular that brought me to his practise, but rather about how I felt and coped with my emotions and state of mind.

I ended up seeing Dr Marco twice a month for the first six months at his home as it was closer for me and most of the time my son Greigan would take me in the early morning to see Dr Marco. He changed my medication and for the first time on mediation, he could grasp my emotions and I could talk openly about the pain I suffered and about my losses.

When I lost the use of my legs, it made me co-dependent and triggered thoughts of wanting to end my life. Percy wanting to leave me triggered another loss I had to deal with but I had not even begun to deal with the trigger of ending my life which I thought I had.

I slowly realised that I ran away from loss and pain. Backed into a corner with nowhere to run, the only option was to take my life.

I had to face every hurt, emotion, and pain head-on. It was as if I had been placed under a massive spotlight with nowhere to hide, I had to stand in the centre of my pain and had to deal with everything I avoided and ran away from.

Nothing about my sessions with Dr Marco were methodical and dealt more with how I felt on that particular day and what the best way was for me to cope.

Some of my sessions were incredibly intense. I cried and sat in the centre of my pain, a perfectly broken woman putting all the pieces of her that she could salvage together again, like a mosaic. Only this time, I chose the pieces to create a better version of me. A more colourful and cheerful me.

I am still a work in progress.

I don't think one really gets to finish the mosaic completely but continue to find new pieces to create a better version of yourself. We are all mosaics, from a distance we form a colourful pattern, but closer we see hundreds of pieces held together. Sometimes the pieces come loose with age and you have to replace it or secure it.

These are life lessons learnt.

There is an Arab on my couch, a friend who is a very wise soul and shared some of his wisdoms and life experiences with me during COVID. What I write further came to realisation with his help.

Thank you, Figo, for your wise words, support, non-judgement and welcoming me into your life. You too taught me a lesson on who you allow into your life, your lesson to me. I knew I was stronger when I let you go at free will as your own life was a journey I wanted no part of so that brief encounter was enlightening.

Figo gave me an Arab name 'Shuruq', which means first light. I can only hope that I can live up to that name and give hope to anyone who comes into my life or gets to hear my life story and can draw knowledge and strength from my experience.

Today is 17 November 2020.

As I am writing this, I look at how far I have come.

I can say with all honesty that the 2020, COVID 19 year was historical. It was then that I realised my true strength and how far I'd come. I understand myself and accept that I am not perfect, but perfectly put together with self-love.

The year 2020 was a purge for the world and my life to rid ourselves of toxic relationships and things that did not add value to our lives or souls.

People come and go in our lives. The secret is not to force anyone to leave or stay but to let them pass through at their own will, as I should have done back in 2017, letting go of Percy.

I have come to realise that you cannot force anything in or out of your life because everything has an expiry date. To force things or relationships into your life can rob you of your peace.

The art of life is to allow it to just flow without stopping or forcing it.

The peace I have now is worth what I have lost.

I have been told that in life, there are no makeovers, but I disagree. We constantly learn from our life experiences and if we are fortunate enough, we can use what we have learnt and apply it to similar situations.

Change is inevitable. Everything in life has an expiry date, from the day we are born to the day we die. It's what we do in between that's important. We should live life to its fullest and leave a lasting impression.

Live your life with purpose and leave people better off when you exit their lives; this is your legacy. We are not all destined for greatness but greatness comes in small acts of kindness that can change a person's life or make it easier.

We are all beautifully broken and put back together perfectly imperfect with love.
Tracy Swinson

Chapter 10
Cancer Carousel

A long-deserved holiday to the beautiful island Zanzibar in Tanzania was exactly what I needed. My soul was in much need of soothing and I needed to quiet my mind after the whirlwind I had come through the past years, but most of all I was hopeful that this holiday would bring a change in Percy and our marriage.

I hoped that Percy and I would be able to reconnect as a couple, rekindle the flame of love we once felt. Matters between us have been unsettling during the last past years. I knew that everything we had been through took a toll on him too and the fact he was nine years younger than me, looking back now I know he was not mentally mature to deal with so much trauma.

I do remember at one stage, giving him a way out without any hard feelings but he refused. I felt excited about us as a couple escaping to an island holiday and the possible reconnection between us instilled me with hope. The feel of tropical sun, smell of the ocean and sunscreen always made me feel sexy.

When the day finally arrived, we were packed and waited in anticipation at the airport to board the plane. I tried to keep the conversation between us upbeat when we had a coffee while waiting but I could not help feeling that there was a barrier where his heart once was. I remained optimistic that maybe things will change when we arrive in Zanzibar. Little did I know my best friend of over 20 year whom I confided in about all we were going through and how I wanted out, she was besotted with Percy and was relaying every conversation to him that I had with her. Little did I know I was playing a chess game that was stacked against me. Ignorance is bliss until it's not. Every woman has her go-to friend that she vents to but not in a million years did I peg my best friend to put the knife in my back.Percy's eyes were dead when I looked into them.

As a paraplegic, I boarded the plane first with assistance of the crew, I was assisted into my seat waiting for Percy, I found it odd when I looked back and saw Percy seated behind me.

How could this be? I thought to myself. We checked in together then I remembered he spoke to the flight attendant when I was wheeled away that is when he must have changed his seat.

It was a pleasant flight. I wasn't going to let seating arrangements ruin the flight there or set the tone. I made friends with a woman who sat next to me, and we struck up a conversation and before landing we exchanged mobile numbers.

Before I knew it, we landed. As we disembarked, the warm tropical air hit us. It felt as if we stepped into sauna. I love the heat and was soaking it all in but Percy complained saying he would never be able to live in heat like this.

The ground crew assisted me off the flight into my wheelchair then wheeled me straight through to get my luggage I thought this was odd I just went straight through customs. Percy on the other hand had to stand in a long que to get through customs. The airport was nothing fancy like a 1st world country.

It was a square brick building dilapidated no fancy scanners or security systems not even air-conditioning. This was a very poor country but the people were humble and friendly, and proud of their country.

On the way to the hotel, the tour guide let us stop along the way to taste some of the fresh fruits. The mangoes were like I have never tasted. One was sweet and juicy, I got so lost in tasting the different fruits when I realised Percy was not really into this. Pity, I think food can be very sexy. Once we arrived at the hotel, we immediately started to explore the resort. Before long, Percy had wandered off on his own mission and I relaxed on my own with a cocktail.

I met some Namibians who were on holiday, and they soon became my holiday friends, we did things together during the day and evenings. I saw very little of Percy except when we had a meal or went to bed at night.

When I lay in bed, I noticed a swelling on my neck just under my ear and thought that perhaps I had a reaction to something I ate. It was not sore, just uncomfortable.

The lump on my neck had grown when I arrived back in South Africa. I went for a check-up at my oncologist and patiently sat waiting for my appointment. I felt unsettled as I always had been when surrounded by other cancer patients awaiting their treatment. This always brought back the memories of what I went through and what I imagined my mum had been through too.

Dr G told me that my blood test looked good and when she examined my neck, suggested that I went for a biopsy to make sure that everything was in order.

I felt anxious and made an appointment as soon as possible. There was a lot going through my mind. My marriage was over; it was clear that Percy had checked out of our relationship a long time ago and I needed see a lawyer to file for divorce.

The sessions with Dr Marco had helped me rebuild the new stronger me and helped me work through what was adding value in my life and what was causing all my anxiety.

I confided in in my best friend at that time and told her what had happened in our lives at home and how unhappy I was. She was always a good sounding board for me and gave her honest opinion on situations but for some reason she seemed distant and I thought that perhaps she was having problems of her own that she did not want to discuss.

As time went on, I got the feeling she was not being sincere I could not put my finger on it. You learn to read a person when you have been friends for 23 years.

I realised that when there is no intimacy in a relationship for years, it is time to move on if your partner doesn't want to work things out.

When I had the biopsy, it was probably the most painful experience I had ever undergone. Not even the operation on my breasts were as painful. After much probing of the lump on my neck, the pathologist finally got a small sample and sent a sample away for testing.

After I waited for a full week for results that seemed to take forever, my oncologist eventually called me and said that she wanted to discuss it in person.

My heart sank. I knew that this was not good news. She would have told me if I was in the clear. I felt like locking myself away in my room and not coming out ever again.

How much more must one go through in this lifetime? I thought to myself. *If I had finished my treatment the first round I would not be going through another biopsy.* All these thoughts whirled around in my head I felt heavy.

Stop this carousal! I want to get off, I thought.

When Percy and I sat opposite Dr G and she started to speak, all I could hear was my heartbeat in my ears.

She told me that I had a deadly tumour which is linked to the breast cancer cells and that she was not hopeful for my recovery because of where it was situated. The tumour was right up against the vagus nerve and pushing up against the main artery supplying blood to the brain it was too large to just go in and remove it without dire consequences (ref of what the vagus nerve's connected to).

Vagus Nerve—Tenth Cranial Nerve.

The vagus nerve, also known as the tenth cranial nerve, cranial nerve X or, simple CNX, is the nerve that interfaces with the parasympathetic control of the heart, lungs and digestive tract.

I could not believe what I heard. Here I was planning on filing for divorce, and now I had to fight for my life once again. I felt as if the universe conspired against me. My faith was put to the test again. On top it, I was turning the big 50.

Percy was occupied on his phone when Dr G explained the procedure for treatment, how they would try to shrink the tumour and then remove it. He might as well not have been there.

I had to make a huge decision about fighting the tumour and felt like I was broken in pieces, knowing that I had to hold it together and be stronger than I had ever been before if I was going to beat this battle.

This time round, I was terrified as I knew what chemotherapy treatments are like but I had only heard how horrific radiation treatments were. I was not sure if I was up to this but I knew I had to give everything I had and toughen up mentally.

I told Dr G that I did not want to know what stage it was on and did not want to be placed in a box.

I convinced myself that everything would be fine, that I would overcome the battle as I overcame worse. Little did I know what waited for me.

We left the consulting rooms and when I got into the car, I turned the radio on and Ironic was playing by Alanis Morressete.

"Fuck my life!" Throwing my hands in the air, the irony was me.

Percy and my friend decided to throw me an early surprise 50th birthday as my treatment started before my birthday. I had no idea that these plans were set in motion as I wrestled with so many feelings of doubt in my head and in my heart.

From being on holiday in Zanzibar in November to being told that I had a deadly tumour in January was a lot to absorb. All I wanted was to be left alone so that I could process it all.

I was reluctant when Percy told me that we were going to a BBQ at my friend's house as I wanted to stay home, but he insisted that we should go and that would be good for me and the kids to get out.

The drive to my friend's place felt eternal. A darkness overcame me. I wanted to crawl into my bed and not be crowded by people. I was still wrestling with the variables of the treatment and a possible poor outcome. Perhaps just living the best life and skip treatment would be better but what would my best life look like spending it going through a divorce?

When we arrived at the house, I noticed that there were a lot of cars parked and knew that I was not able to deal with so many people, but it was too late. I smiled as we entered the house and realised that I was ambushed into my surprise 50th birthday party.

I was angry but could not show it but everything in me was screaming for the world and noise in my head to stop so I could collect myself and my thoughts.

How could Percy and my friend be so insensitive to throw me into this situation so soon after receiving dreadful news? I thought.

I smiled like I'd always done until my kids gave me a toast, which caused me to fall apart. Nicole comforted me, realising that the battle that lay ahead would have to be fought tooth-and-nail.

My kids put on their brave faces that evening. Although I could see the panic in their eyes, there was nothing I could do to make it better. I accepted the severity of my condition. This was not a fifty/fifty situation this was the difference between life and death, what lay in the balance was the latter according to my doctor.

When we headed home, I wanted to be left alone with my thoughts of how I was going to fight the tumour physically and emotionally. I needed to get my head in the right space.

I sat in the coffee shop and listened to music as I waited for the chemicals to be infused into my bloodstream to fight the tumour on my neck. I remember as I watched the nurse secure the red devil drip and placed the needle into the biggest vein she could find.

Doxorubicin, an old chemotherapy drug that carries this unusual moniker because of its distinctive hue and fearsome toxicity, remains a key treatment for many cancer patients. (Red Devil)

I shut my eyes as she opened the drip and prayed that it was going to be effective and that everything would work out for the best.

Three sessions in, the chemo did not work, and the tumour had grown.

Dr G was concerned and suggested that there was another chemo we could try and warned me that the side effects were harsh. I Google researched the Cisplatin treatment, a type of chemotherapy that destroys quickly dividing cells, such as cancer cells, and decided to take my chances. The side effects were harsh however it was minor to having to live your life going forward.

The weekly chemo treatment commenced. I soon lost all my hair and was a lighter shade of grey. Some days, the pain was intolerable, and I battled at work, which was not doing so well either.

My son and his friend were both in their first year of university studying law and decided to help me out at Khula Placements to keep my business in shape. The days I felt like I had energy to work, *I would make it to my office then lay with my head on my desk*, I thought to myself if you can make it to your desk you still have it in you to fight.

Three months later, the tumour that was propped up against my vagus nerve that pushed up against the main artery in my neck had shrunk sufficiently for specialists to operate and remove.

I was nervous when I lay on the operating table and knew that one wrong move would result in paralysis on the right-hand side of my face. I woke up two hours later with the great news that the whole tumour was removed successfully and that I was able to move the muscles in my face.

I lay in the ward on my own feeling so grateful for small mercies. I could take a breather now and move on to the next challenge.

The battle was not yet conquered. I had to undergo further chemo and radiation treatment for the next six months. This was where the actual fight started.

Still not out of the woods, I was given a short break of a month before going into my next lot of treatment. During this time, the situation between Percy and myself worsened so I booked myself into a hotel for five days.

149

I needed to clear my head and make a decision to stay with Percy or leave him as my gut told me that he had interests elsewhere. I was in pure survival mode not just to fight cancer but my life going forward needed to change.

I chose that if I was strong enough after my treatment, I would tell Percy that I wanted out of our loveless marriage. There had not been any physical intimacy for years and I saw no point in prolonging the inevitable.

But first, I had to face the next six months of treatment that awaited me.

The treatments began with back-to-back radiation treatment, with chemo treatment once a week. I listened to the radiation oncologist explain the process forward and what the side effects would be.

One of the side effects is that I could possibly get another tumour elsewhere at a later stage. At this point, I though well I have managed to poison my body this far stopping now would be in vain. I could not worry about the what-ifs in the future I needed to deal with the present.

My body needed to be poisoned for me to live, I thought.

Percy had checked out at this point that the one afternoon at radiotherapy, I had passed out in my chair. A doctor came up to him and asked him if he had noticed I was passed out.

Percy replied, "She is always passing out, she will come round."

That afternoon, the doctor put the number of a social worker in my hand and said I should get assistance. Percy was cold towards me; there was no compassion in his eyes. It was more like I was a burden and I felt sad that I was the burden.

They lay me down to fit my mould for the radiation tunnel and heated a plastic mesh that was placed over my face, neck, and chest. Once it had set, they clipped it down to ensure that it was secure. I kept telling myself to breathe as I hated confined spaces and now had aluminium green mesh that suffocated me.

After this procedure had taken place, the daily radiation treatment started, followed by chemo once a week.

On my first day of radiation, they clipped me down with the mesh mould. I could not move as a robotic arm moved across my head, then down to where the tumour had once made a home for itself. The radiation blasted the area while I lay with my eyes shut. It sounded like a wind tunnel.

While I lay pinned down onto the table with my eyes closed trying to take my mind off what was really going on, I would have conversations with God in this time nothing in particular but like I would talk to my mother. I found much comfort in the fifteen-minute conversation. I was not angry, I was humbled with my conversations.

I was done in fifteen minutes and on my way back home before I had to return day after day for further onslaughts.

The constant feeling of being completely depleted grew worse. One morning, I knew that something was wrong as I experienced a pain I had not felt before. My back ached and it felt like I was running a temperature and it felt like my organs were shutting down, I was shivering despite this temperature.

Elizabeth, my caregiver, called Percy and told him that he needed to take me to the hospital as soon as possible, but he was in no rush and only arrived later that afternoon. It was clear that I caused him an inconvenience, as he had to drop whatever he was doing to assist me.

I was admitted to the Donald Gordon where Percy left me in admissions and went back home.

Everything went dark.

I woke up in ICU with acute renal failure and had to stay there for a week, without Percy visiting me. When they moved me into a ward, my body did not recover, and I had to receive transfusions to boost my system. Three transfusions later, I was placed in isolation and only received one visit from Percy as we had had an argument prior and he disconnected.

One morning, a social worker arrived and wanted to ask me a few questions. I think my oncologist called this meeting as she was concerned that I had not received the support I needed and was under-nourished. My eldest son was called in during our next meeting to discuss my treatment plan going forward as Percy had checked out completely.

I ended up taking an uber with my caregiver to treatment and back as I had no other support. This made me more determined than ever to win my battle and walk away contented and sane.

I counted down the treatments. Every time I lay on the radiation table, I closed my eyes and prayed.

It was my only hope to hold on to.

I can honestly say that I felt like a walking pin cushion during the treatment and have never been poked and prodded by so many needles in one year.

I was elated to leave the battlefield. I would not look back. I fought bravely and lived. I survived a year of physical torture and an emotional roller coaster.

When I went through treatment, my business was on the brink of failing and very little revenue was being made.

I had to say goodbye to my Nicole as she made her way to Miami with her fiancé to work on a cruise line. I told her that I would be filing for a divorce. She was so happy that I had made the decision to move on with my life and find some peace. I sat at the airport and held my beautiful, strong, and courageous daughter and waved goodbye as she took a step into a new adventure of her life.

It was bittersweet. I felt proud of the wonderful person she became despite any hardships she had experienced growing up when I was shot, she was hijacked, faced another armed robbery, and watched her mother survived two bouts of cancer. What a strong person she turned out to be.

The anchor has now been lifted and Nicole embarked on a journey of her own. As a mother, you never want your children to go through such extreme trauma in their lives. I am so proud of all three of my children how they have come through all this.

As a parent, you make decisions the best you can and your children are always at the forefront but not all decisions are the right ones and end up impacting your life and the lives around you.

I often wondered what my life would have looked like if I never entertained that wrong number. I know deep down they are still dealing with the hand that life dealt them but they are cut from my cloth and are fighters too.

I believe it was grit and God's grace that embraced me through an awful year where I faced death.

I live each day with gratitude.

I was done with this cancer carousel and ready for a new chapter.

Little did I know that I was walking into a minefield.

She Fights.

Born into a world she will never understand. She is hopeful and dreams a dream. A lust for life is what she was taught. Death is what she was dealt. She fights like a Knight. Once, twice, three or more. What is this life for? The fight is for life. She fights like a Knight.

Tracy Swinson

Chapter 11
Coming Clean in COVID

When I surfaced 2019 where I felt invincible, 2020 promised to be a year where I would be able to get my life back on track and set new goals and plans in action to move forward with renewed enthusiasm.

I hated the watered-down version of myself I had become and made a firm decision to de-clutter my life, which included my failed marriage and the toxic people in my life.

My main goal was to get Tracy back in action.

Back in my office, I gathered the remains of my ruined business off the floor. This was not easy as I had to deal with my divorce as well.

I received legal advice on what steps I needed to take to leave Percy and spoke to a good friend about how unhappy I was.

My instinct was telling me that Percy was unfaithful to me. One plus one does not add up to five. Our marriage was over. Trying to get it back to where it had been, to its moments of joy and bliss, was like rowing a boat with one ore in the water, going around endlessly in circles.

I knew that Percy was up to something and needed clarity. He was mostly on the prowl and crawled back at 4 am in the morning. Some nights, he wreaked of booze and smelt funky.

One evening when he snuck in and headed straight for the bathroom, I could smell that odd odour. I continued to casually dish-up dinner and kept to myself. Still, I felt battered black and blue emotionally, knowing that it was better to say nothing and avoid a heated confrontation.

After dinner, Percy went to have a bath. When I brushed my teeth before heading to off to bed, I wiped my mouth on a towel and smelt that funky smell. I gagged. Now, it was on my hand towel as well as on my mouth.

It had gone too far. Furious, I needed to address the issue and asked Percy to get out of the bath so that we could have a talk. He refused to budge and get out of the bath and nonchalantly asked me what my problem was.

I told him about *that* smell that had now pervaded my towel. He kept silent so I left and put the towel on his pillow as I went to sleep.

Percy was passive-aggressive towards me the following morning and angered about my implication that he had been sleeping around. I asked him about that smell as it had not been there on weekends and only during the week when he went out.

He told me that he had a bladder infection.

When I called his mother Joan about this, she suggested that I should book an appointment for him at the doctor. I told Percy that his mother and I were concerned about the infection he had for longer than a month and he exploded, yelling at me, accusing me of trying to catch him out, and refused to go and see a doctor.

I finally had my answer, totally unaware that my best friend had leaked every conversation I had with her about Percy to him. At this point, I could not care less. Everything I had said was truthful.

I know now that the decay had set in shortly after I was shot, going from an able body to a paraplegic it is a lot to absorb especially from my husband's point of view. I tried to keep the spark and the intimacy going even though I knew it was now different.

As the years went by, there were long periods where we were not intimate as much as I tried to rekindle that spark through roll play and provocative lingerie, he just wasn't interested. This broke my confidence completely. I already had body issues, losing use of my leg and then my breasts.

When we were intimate, the only way I could describe the encounters was angry sex. It got more and more rough as time went by, shoving my face into a pillow taking and fist full of hair so I could not breathe. In my mind, I was saying no and wanted him to stop. One afternoon, it was the worst of all occasions, I bled for days and I could not help feeling violated and transporting me back to the night of my rape.

I knew he was watching a lot of porn and it seem to get worse over the years. I eventually stopped wanting to have sex with him so I would only give him oral sex which became rough and violent too that I would have bruising around my mouth for days. It broke my heart that there were not tender loving intimate moments in our marriage anymore.

An explosion of raw emotions and heated arguments began.

I told Percy that I wanted out of the marriage. He said that he was done with the accusations I threw at him about sleeping around. It's not difficult to fathom the truth when a married man is always armed with condoms.

I was done with Percy's denials and had lost my voice and inner strength to contest him. It was time for a change and had to take care of my own life.

In February 2020, Percy booked a holiday for us in Cape Town.

Although I went with him reluctantly against my better judgement, knowing that it would be a waste of time, it was clear within a few days that we could not tolerate being in each other's space.

The final straw was when we were crossing the road at the Victoria Alfred Waterfront in Cape Town my wheelchair wheel clipped part of the cobble paving when crossing the road and I fell forward into oncoming traffic. Percy just carried on walking and tourists came to my assistance. At this point, I was done; no going back. Whatever feelings I had, were dead and buried.

I needed to go home. He also had to get back home as his father was dying from cancer.

Back home, he left to see his father and I was relieved to have the house for myself, happy to be alone as I wanted my life to be. When he returned two weeks later, he wanted to know if I really wanted to end our marriage. I could sense that he wanted me to say that it was not what I wanted, but I was definitely done.

Emotional abuse is far worse than physical exploitation. Percy had never lifted a hand to me or hurt me deliberately, but his emotional abuse was as clear as daylight.

My head whirled.

Our world tumbled into a pandemic called COVID, and our President announced lockdown as I received my divorce papers from Percy which were filed on my birthday and having my son Greigan, who was studying for his LLB, still living with me.

Greigan packed up his room and told me that he was moving out as Percy had become verbally abusive towards him when I was closed in at my office. It broke my heart to say goodbye to him, but I knew that it was best as I saw that the divorce was going to be acrimonious and a fight brewed.

With my business shut down, divorce on its way and locked down with my soon to be ex, it was the quiet before the storm.

What promised to be a new adventure resulted in my world being turned upside down with the rest of the world. I was terrified of catching COVID as I had just finished my chemo radiation treatment and it would have been ironic if I died from catching the flu.

There I was, stuck in the house with Percy, the very person I was trying to get away from. I moved into my son's room to get out of his way and stay clear of him.

Percy fired Elisabeth, our domestic and my caregiver, and decided that he would do the cooking and clean the house. I tried to reason with him that I needed my caregiver to help me bath and keep the house hygienic but he refused to listen. I soon adapted but with great difficulty I decided to clean what I could but could not manage a huge house.

As I wheeled myself to the kitchen one day, Percy gave me a look that chilled me to the bone and I asked him what was wrong.

"I never hated anyone as much as I hate you," he spewed. "There's a thin line between love and hate," I said.

I could not recall having ever hated anyone as he had explained to me, convinced that he felt that way because I did not want to accept his offer for the divorce.

He wanted to offer me half the furniture and half the value of the house which was nothing as he had taken an extension on the bond to buy himself a car and the market was down being in the middle of COVID.

Conversations flew back and forth between us. He tried to be cordial, but I knew that there was a volcano waiting to erupt. I had to rely on him to help me bath, which he stopped doing, so I went for days without bathing.

Percy made it as difficult for me as he possibly could.

My business was shut down and I had no money to pay any bills. Although I had helped him with money many times over during our marriage, the favour was not returned.

There was nothing I could do. I had no idea how long the COVID lockdown would last and got involved with Personal Protective Equipment products to secure an income.

I did not feel my best and lost weight fast.

I was determined to see the divorce through, as well as coming to terms with the new regulations of masks and sanitisers.

Percy would not allow me in the kitchen to cook so I took the back seat. One evening, he gave me a burger and I politely thanked him. I wasn't hungry and had constant pains in my stomach, so I placed it next to me and continued to watch television.

My German shepherd Bella grabbed the burger off the plate and devoured it. I told her off but was relieved as I was not that hungry. When I went to bed later that evening, Percy tried to console Bella who was vomiting and brought up bile. I could not help put think that there was something wrong with the burger that was meant for me but waved it off as a coincidence.

COVID was at a peak, yet Percy was out of the house for hours, returning with items from the store. I panicked. Then I heard him talk to someone and realised that he was out visiting friends.

I told him that it was irresponsible and even shared posts on Facebook that asked people to keep to the COVID lockdown rules and not put their families and friends at risk by socialising.

I did not mention that it was the case at my house, but two days later received a cease-and-desist notice demanding that I had to immediately stop an illegal or allegedly illegal activity.

I was furious. 19-years-of-marriage has turned ugly. *Or had it always been this way and I did not see it?* I thought.

I had lost so much weight that none of my clothes fitted me and had no idea what was happening to me.

To make some money to settle bills, I hustled during the day, but it was not that lucrative, and creditors started bugging me.

The only thing that remained steady was my firm decision to leave Percy.

Resolute that there was a better life that would greet me on the other side of the battlefield, I took good advice from a friend to write a book about what had happened to me while everything was still fresh in my mind. She was keen to help me get my book published so jumped into writing my story.

Day after day, it became increasingly difficult to live with Percy. He became more and more passive-aggressive in his approach towards me. I felt unsafe and unsure, the tension in the house had become progressively palatable and I had to do everything within my power to avoid the slightest confrontation.

It had almost been a week since my last bath and when I asked Percy one morning to please help me, he reluctantly agreed much later that afternoon with a heavy sigh.

I got undressed in the bedroom and waited patiently for him and called to him. When he eventually came into the room, he gave me that same look of hatred and loathing as he'd done when he told me how much he hated me. When he lifted me, I knew that he was going to hurt me. I was not wrong.

Percy whipped me off the bed and walked over to bath and just threw me into the tub. Instinctively I put my arms out to break my fall and I landed in the bath, water splashed out.

I looked at Percy with tears in my eyes and said, "Please don't be so rough with me."

He threw me that loathing look and said, "Get out of the bath by yourself, you fucking bitch!" and picked up his keys as he left the house, shutting the door with a loud bang.

I sat alone in the bathtub. Miserable, with no phone, no towel, and no way of getting out of the bath on my own. I wept, my body ached all over and I had a cut on my elbow.

The man I thought loved me, and whom I respected as a gentleman who'd never harm me physically, had just crossed the line and destroyed the little faith I had left of him.

A zillion thoughts zoomed through my mind. I felt violated. An abused woman.

Abandoned in the tub, I decided to make the most of it and settled down, soaking there for more than an hour, then pulled the plug and waited. I hoped that he would return, but the house was silent, and I had to stay in the tub as another hour passed slowly.

Panic set in as I realised that I could not get out of the tub, and I was freezing as it was the middle of winter.

When I heard my next-door neighbour talk to her children, I was about to call her, but heard Percy stomp into the house, and called to him.

He came to the bathroom and stood in the doorway, looking at me.

I asked him to please help me.

"Sure, your highness," he sneered sarcastically. "Is there anything else the princess needs?"

I remained quiet and calm and told him I was ready.

He roughly lifted me out of the bath and dumped me on the bed.

I asked him to please shut the door, which he did with a bang, leaving me in tears.

I called my aunt Cynthia and told her what had occurred, how my elbow bled and that my body was in pain from the plunge into the tub. Concerned about well-being and safety as Percy became more and more passively aggressive towards me and now was abusive, she advised me to contact my lawyer.

When I told my lawyer about the abuse, he told me to approach the courts, an open a protection order against Percy as our divorce proceedings hadn't begun yet.

There was no indication as to when lockdown would end and being trapped in a house with an abusive spouse who could do to me whatever pleased him, it was not a safe environment.

I lay in tears in bed that night.

I found it difficult to comprehend how two people who once cared and loved each other, could turn so hateful towards each other. I was no stranger to abuse as my previous marriage suffered the same fate.

Beaten while pregnant with Nicole and given birth to her with black eye, chocked out, pinned up against the gate with his car, picked up and thrown across the room. Emotional abuse of being told I was fat and looked like a beached whale when I was pregnant. That lead to many insecurities.

All I knew was that I had to stay clear of Percy and the courts had granted the protection order.

Percy was furious when the police arrived and served the protection order. He even had the audacity to tell the police get off *his* property as it was *his* house. They quickly put him in his place, telling him that it was a protection order and that he had no right to make any demands.

I also notified the court about an unlicensed firearm. When the police requested that he hand over the gun, he denied that it even existed. They told him that whatever he had in the form of a weapon needed to be handed over. When they found a huge hunting knife, knuckleduster, and switchblade, they confiscated it and escorted Percy to the police station.

An hour later, the police arrived with Percy and allowed him to pack clothes and some of his belongings, then marched him off the premises, unfortunately forgetting to take the house keys from him.

I stayed clear of the confrontation and feared my safety, even with the police being there. I knew what Percy was capable of doing.

Like that, he was gone from the house. How I was going to survive with no money did not matter. The important thing was that I was safe and sound.

My first night alone was strangely peaceful. For the first time, I felt like I wasn't living on eggshells.

My dad had arranged for a friend of his to come and stay on the premises. An ex-cop with lots of protection experience, Gerrie was an old grey-headed man.

Percy moved in with a good friend of his for a few months then I believe he moved in with his girlfriend.

I felt safe with Percy not living there.

I welcomed my Elisabeth back, who could help me to pack up Percy's belongings, with Gerrie bearing witness that no vandalism or theft incurred to his belongings.

It took us nearly a day to pack Percy's clothes from the cupboard into boxes.

What happened next, I would never have imagined in a million years. To Elizabeth's shock and my and Gerrie's amusement, she uncovered heaps of explicit pornographic DVDs and magazines, as well as a purple vibrator and other kinky paraphernalia.

I was amazed and thought in disbelief how I was married to a man for 19-years, who always told me how disgusting and appalling he found pornography. Now that I stared at his porno treasure chest, blood drained from my face as it struck me how little I knew of him, that he was a complete stranger to me.

How is it possible to be with someone for so many years and have no idea what dirty secrets that person hides? I thought with tears in my eyes. *Do you really know the person that you share your life with? What they hide from you?*

I had always been aware that Percy kept some secrets from me, that he might have visited porno sites like most men do, but never thought that it would unveil a porn stash. What came out of Percy's cupboard was something I was not prepared for.

We loaded all Percy's stuff on the back of Gerrie's bakkie, except for his *dirty secret*, which I kept as evidence. Gerrie dropped Percy's clothes at Joan's house, who was rather inquisitive as to who the *strange man* was.

While Gerrie, an ex-policeman, was staying in the house with me in the beginning of when the court battles had started. He was there as a protective measure as there was no electricity and the electric fence was not working.

It was mentally and emotionally tiring, with affidavits being answered and returned for re-reading, and took a toll on me. There were some nights that I would cry myself to sleep.

There was no going back, I knew I had to see this through.

I was terrified when a date was set for the protection order to be heard in court. It was the first time that I would see Percy since he was marched off the property by the police.

After waiting for hours, we were told that Percy could not make it and the case was postponed, and a new court date was set and so we had to wait another two months.

During this time, I did not feel very safe when Gerrie moved out and I was on my own again.

The affidavits and the accusations that Percy made were so absurd. He desperately tried to defend his actions. His inconsistency and lies in the affidavits became very apparent.

We were back at court and once again it was postponed. The court case was postponed five times.

During the time I waited patiently for this court case to take place, I applied for interim maintenance. It was the hardest time of my life as Percy made sure that I was left with absolutely nothing.

He had cut the Wi-Fi, cancelled Netflix he had even discontinued the electricity. There was no food in the fridge and had no idea where my next meal was coming from.

Still, I knew that I needed to see this through.

One afternoon, my neighbour Tina popped in to see how I was doing and when she found that there was no electricity in the house, she fitted a cable through from her house to my house so that I was able to at least keep the fridge on and make myself a cup of tea.

Tina's visits became a regular thing. She brought me cooked meals and make sure that I was okay.

I was isolated from everybody. Nicole was living in the UK and could do nothing to assist me and being under lockdown, my sons were unable to visit.

To make matters worse, that little cut I had on my elbow from when Percy threw me in the bath had become infected so badly that it had turned septic. I ran a dangerously high temperature.

Tina called an ambulance and I ended up in Rose Acres Hospital where they put me on a drip immediately and told me that they needed to operate on my elbow as they cut away the tissue that had turned necrotic and if they did not remove the infected tissue, I could lose my arm.

I underwent surgery the following morning. They cut away a large amount of tissue from an elbow that exposed my elbow joint.

Here I was in the middle of COVID during lockdown recovering from what was just a small cut initially but resulted in a gaping hole in my elbow where there was not flesh but now the bone was exposed. The healing of my elbow was going to take time and many trips between home and the wound clinic to make sure that this wound did not get infected any further and healed properly.

My friend Michelle made special trips during her day to get me to the clinic and back to make sure the wound was cleaned and dressed so it could heal.

Tina, I would say, is definitely an earth angel. She selflessly checked up on me every day to make sure I was okay. Days when I was too weak to bath myself, Tina and her daughter would assist me in and out of the bath. Tina made sure that I had company and even invited me to have a Sunday lunch with them and if it wasn't a meal, it was always a cup of coffee and a good laugh.

We kept each other company quite often, especially in the evenings. We would sit for hours just talking and laughing and forgetting about the fact we were in the middle of COVID. We would find something to entertain ourselves, to discuss and laugh about. Tina is a true friend in every sense of the word.

The legal battle bounced back and forth back and forth. It was exhausting.

Thankfully, I had assistance from my aunt Cynthia with the affidavits, she answered them factually and not emotionally. That's how the courts operate, they don't care about the emotion of why a person is going through a divorce, but focus on the facts.

There were a lot of accusations that were cast back and forth but I did not take the bait and just sat back, let Percy hang himself. He was a compulsive liar and that the courts would catch him out eventually. In the middle of all of this, there was an unlicensed firearm that was brushed over. No real notice was taken to this even though we had highlighted the fact that he was in possession of an unlicensed firearm.

Percy counter acted with an affidavit that stated he had handed the gun in to a gun shop in 2016, which was not true as I attempted to commit suicide with that very gun in 2017. The courts were more interested in getting the protection order put in place and not following through on where the gun was.

Percy knew that if the courts focused on this gun and doing a full investigation he would get a minimum of seven years in jail for an unlicensed firearm. Needless to say, till date, no further investigation has been done with regards to that unlicensed firearm as to where it is.

We were back at the domestic violence case and once again Percy had not arrived at court but sent his lawyer to say he was out of town and could not make it to court. Something deep inside of me knew that this was a lie.

Tina was with us that day at the court as a witness and went outside to dial Percy's company number. When she asked for Percy, the receptionist said that he was out at a client and would be back later and confirmed he actually was in town.

My advocate Derek stood with Tina when she made the call on speaker phone and he heard what the receptionist told Tina.

The case was postponed. I was completely in awe that this happened for a fifth time without any results. I needed to do something about it.

Back at Tina's house, she cooked us a meal and we chatted about the case that should have come to an end a long time ago. If we could prove that Percy was in town, we could get the court to make a ruling.

I phoned friends of mine who worked in the security industry and asked them if they could help me confirm that Percy was in town. They asked me for his car registration number.

Tina and I were having dinner when my friend from the security company called back and confirmed that they had photographs of Percy in town on the day he should have been in court. I informed Derek that I had evidence that Percy lied and was in contempt of court.

At our next court date, Derek did not take any nonsense from Percy or his lawyer. He suggested that we should settle out of court because if we didn't, Percy would be going to jail.

Derek told Percy's lawyer that she would be disbarred for covering up for his client, and that Percy would definitely be going to jail for contempt of court as we had concrete evidence, and proposed that the protection order should be made permanent, and that he paid 10 000 to cover our fees.

Percy's lawyer accepted as Percy did not want to face the magistrate as he knew that he was in the wrong and would be penalised and jailed.

We were victorious. I felt safe knowing that Percy was not allowed within one kilometre of me for the rest of my life.

It was only one obstacle I had overcome, there were many more to face: I was jobless, penniless, without electricity and had to rely on Tina for food, or Nicole's mother-in-law to occasionally drop off some groceries.

It wasn't that important for me to not have food, as long as my dogs and cats were fed, I was content. Percy didn't even care that the animals were affected by his actions too.

Another battle greeted me, I had to get interim maintenance paid that would help me through the period while waiting for the divorce to go through. When we submitted our financial disclosures, I had nothing to hide and I put forward my bank statements. My earnings were minimal. Percy lied about his earnings as he'd move money and hide assets.

I told Derek that we should take action as soon as possible as Percy would do whatever he could to ensure that it looked as if he had absolutely no money.

Fortunately, my advocate was sharp and knew exactly how to deal with the nonsense Percy had served up in the form of a bank statement.

While all the back and forth paperwork between the lawyers and myself, I also visited the wound clinic, with Michelle assisting me every third day. The wound was irrigated and covered up again. It was an arduous process but it needed to be done.

I had also lost so much weight that I barely fitted into anything. Fortunately, Michelle was the same size as I was and in the goodness of heart gave me clothes so that I could look decent as well. It didn't make much of a difference. Anyone could see that how worn-out and tired I was and literally hung on a thread.

Percy had successfully turned his mother against me. The woman I considered my mother, whom I spent copious amounts of time with to make her feel that she was part of the family, and Percy's brother—who he'd never spoken to for 20 years—I accepted as family. I was the glue that held their families together. Since the divorce proceeding began, I became the villain.

Blood is thicker than water. When you go through a divorce, people pick a side. Nobody ever sits on the same fence.

A good friend of mine, who I had confided in and me and my kids regarded as family, betrayed me and was no longer a name that would even cross our lips.

I blocked her and her family on every social media platform and never to talk about them again. That kind of betrayal is unforgivable.

It was early December when the interim court case to be heard. My advocate had done her work thoroughly with a lot of help from me and my investigative skills. We uncovered quite a lot. Percy claimed that he had absolutely no money but had managed to afford 25,000 grand to have two full sleeves of tattoos done.

I sat quietly in court while the advocates bickered back and forth with arguments and counter arguments. Percy didn't look up once, he was occupied on his phone, obviously chatting to whoever on WhatsApp, which was not allowed in court while a case was in motion.

My advocate declared that bank statements of over 100 000 Grand was unaccounted for.

The magistrate stared at Percy, waiting for him to lift his head. He did not budge and carried on with his phone messaging. The magistrate was not impressed and stated at the end of the court case that she would deliberate and go through her notes, she would make a fair decision and would have a ruling by mid-December.

I so desperately needed the magistrate to be on my side just so that I could have enough money to buy food. I knew that COVID would come to end sometime and that I would be able to get back to work.

I battled to afford to feed myself, let alone my cats and my dog and had to ask Derek. I then asked for my lawyer to make arrangements for our beautiful German shepherd to stay with Percy as I was unable to take care of her. I could manage to feed my two small cats but the Bella cost way too much money and at that stage.

Percy had also cancelled the medical aid so I was unable to continue my post-chemo treatment let alone going for check-ups with my oncologist. Derek fought desperately for Percy to put me back on the medical aid which he did only for a while but cancelled it after a few months he was ruthless like that.

I was then able unable to continue with my treatment and could not fathom how this man who had spent 19 years with me could be so cruel and so unkind. It was a mutual decision to leave each other. What was clear now was that he didn't love me, which was understandable, but his cruelty was beyond reason.

During mid-December, I spent a weekend with my best friend Adele who lived in Randburg. We laughed and chatted, sitting underneath the stars when a WhatsApp came through from the court, informing me that Percy had lost the court case and was instructed to pay me maintenance of 11,000 Grand a month as well as my medical aid. I had to stop taking my post-chemo treatment tablets when Percy took me off the medical aid so I was relieved that I could continue the treatment.

I was so relieved. Finally, I could fend for myself and not rely on Tina to keep buying me food and taking care of me. For the first time, I could take care of myself and even treat Tina to a lunch or two.

It was one small victory to start, now it was time to get this divorce out of the way.

In spite of everything going on the legal side, I felt free. The old Tracy that I knew was making her way back and it felt great.

I was even asked to do an inspirational talk for an NPO which I thoroughly enjoyed. I think this for me was a taste of things to come to inspire people to push forward even when it feels hopeless.

Being in a wheelchair, fifty-two years old, and starting my life all over again was something, I would never have even imagined I would be doing.

But here I am. This was my reality.

It was stressful but I was happy and at peace.

She didn't see it
But she morphed
Into a butterfly!
Tracy Swinson

Chapter 12
Love and Rose-Coloured Glasses

Let's back up a little.

I kept a brave face on as I waited for my divorce to be finalised. I yearned to let go of 19-years of marriage and make sense of what went wrong, where I went wrong. At this point, I felt like I had been put on a spin cycle with rocks. I was battered and bruised emotionally and physically.

I blamed myself for many years for the state of my marriage but Dr Marco reminded me that it takes both parties to make a marriage work and me going to marriage counselling is like having only one ore in the water you just go around in circles. I believe emotional abuse is far worse than physical it takes a very long time to heal and even when you have healed, I don't think you ever give yourself completely.

While I was trying to pick up the pieces and make sense of the last nineteen years, Percy had moved on really fast and was now living with his new girlfriend. I needed to move on, too.

Let's talk about love and rose-coloured glasses.

As I started to write this book and ended up in this chapter, the saying "hindsight is 20/20," well that is the honest truth.

I decided to go back to the beginning and retrace my footsteps to see if I had missed some clues.

That night, I dialled the wrong telephone number and got through to Percy's phone was mistake number one. Entertaining his charming calls without ever meeting him was my second mistake.

For some reason, I always see the best in people. My children are convinced my BS radar does not work on the men I fell in love with and have assured me that they would be involved with any relationships going forward. Heaven forbid! I can only imagine it will be like the first guy that came to take my daughter out on a date it was like the Spanish inquisition, the poor guy after that first date never dared to come near Nicole.

Percy told me that he had a successful business and drove a convertible Audi. The truth of the matter was that he lied. The car belonged to a lawyer friend of his and even that friendship was a little shady, while unpacking a cupboard I found a photo of Percy and this friend with his hands on her breasts and yet she was a married woman. I did question him, he said they were just friends but I never truly believed it and later my daughter commented on it too. The signs were there the whole time but rose glasses.

How was I to know the truth until I had met him? By then it was too late as we had developed a unique bond. It was not about material things but the truth.

When I saw his dilapidated car, I made up an excuse in my head. When I asked him about his convertible, he avoided answering me. It was a massive red flag, but I chose to ignore it.

Dumb. I know!

When I lived in Durban and he came to visit me, he booked a night at the Hilton hotel. When they requested a credit card for secure payment, he told them that he did not have one and would prefer to pay in cash. I used my credit card and said that we would settle the money in the morning. After we checked out the following morning, Percy went to draw cash and came back telling me that the ATM had swallowed his card and that he would deposit the money into my account.

I felt embarrassed and told him that I would put it on my card and ended up paying for his flight back to Johannesburg, telling him that I would loan him the money. While he was packing and I cleaned the room, I found his ATM card tucked into the side of his bag and realised that it was never swallowed at the ATM. I made another excuse for him and just kept quiet instead of confronting him as I did not want to embarrass him.

These were some of the red flags that should have been enough for me to end our relationship but by then, I had fallen for him and chose not to see the flags.

I thought it was a carnival and wanted to go on this crazy ride. And my, was it a crazy ride filled with lies and deceit. The truth he was a liar!

Three months into the marriage, I had to go back to Durban to wrap up the sale of my house. Instinctively, I had a strange feeling that all was not what it seemed to be. When I returned home early from Durban, I found his mobile and for some reason checked his phone and found 20 SMSs from the ex-girlfriend he had spent the weekend flirting with.

I know that at this point, you would ask why did I not leave him?

The honest answer is that I don't know. All I know for certain is that it only got worse during the years that followed.

Now, we are stuck in an acrimonious divorce. Percy had already moved on and was living with the new girlfriend and me, I was fighting for what little remained of my life.

The court date for our divorce eventually arrived and I felt like I had just stepped off this carnival ride. I was sick to my stomach and just wanted this all to end.

My advocate cut a deal with Percy to pay me two years rehabilitative maintenance to get me back on my feet. I knew that this was not the best settlement, but I was done. I could not go another year of court cases. Two years of it was more than enough.Till date, the estate has not been split and he has transferred the car into his girlfriend's name and hid whatever assets we had. My son, Greigan, is currently trying to get the little bit of pension that I am entitled to. He has not kept to the court order paying maintenance and I am trying to find him to get payment before I get evicted out of my home. Getting my business or a job has been extremely challenging. But I have believed it's always darkest before the light and good things are on the horizon.

The day our divorce went though, I decided to spend my Christmas with my cousin in Cape Town. Shortly before I was to return to Johannesburg, I caught COVID and so did my cousin. During the two weeks of solitude, I decided to move to Cape Town. I have always found peace in this city.

When I recovered from COVID, I packed up my flat and moved to Cape Town lock stock-and-barrel. While waiting for my things to arrive, I stayed with my cousin at her home and I am so grateful for her taking me in during this time. While staying with her, my wheelchair scrapped her skirtings in her beautiful home which I felt terrible about. This was later remedied with compensation of sandpaper and paint.

It was a humble start, but my view was breath-taking.

The peace I have now is worth what I lost. Being single at fifty-three is not a bad thing. It is good for the soul.

I am yet to get my business up and running. Time is ticking but my priority was to write my story as this cloud has a silver lining.

The amount of strength and resilience it took me to get through the pandemic, physical abuse, divorce and moving provinces, all I can do is sit here with a smile on my face and tell you I made it.

If you are going through a tough time, hang in there. You too can do it. You are Unbreakable too.

I am pretty sure that by now you would be questioning love and intimacy going forward?

Yes, I had not been in an intimate relationship in years and the lockdown made it impossible to meet anyone. Being a paraplegic also makes it hard to put yourself out there as it is going to take someone very special to take on a woman with a disability.

I had no desire to really meet anyone or have another man in my space. I just wanted to make friends and enjoy my freedom. Being tied down so soon after marriage of nineteen years just did not seem logical.

I needed to work on myself and heal my broken heart.

My physical disability does not take away from the fact I am a woman with desires and still have the need to be touched and made love to.

My friends suggested I should put myself out there and join a dating website. Then to push the envelope, I was challenged to do 30 dates and write about my experience of what life looked like after fifty and back on the market.

Challenge accepted!

Don't get me wrong, I was certainly not looking for love, but my curiosity was roused. I needed to see what my market value was. After a long marriage, I no longer felt desirable.

'If my husband didn't want me who would?' I questioned.

Accepting this social experiment, I had to keep my guard up as many dates could get messy.

I sat with a glass of wine in the one hand and my phone in the other registering on two dating apps. I looked a mess. My hair was up, and I had joggers on with no make-up. That was fine as we were in the middle of a pandemic.

Michelle and I were best friends and did a lot together.

One night, she told me to get dressed as we were going out to a pub. In the nineteen years I lived in the area, I had never been out to a local pub, so this was going to be interesting. In fact, I had never been on a ladies' night in all the time I was married.

172

We arrived at this dodgy smoked-filled pub that had a pool table in the middle of the floor and a small dance floor where a band was playing.

This was really not my scene, I thought, knowing that I would need a few tequilas to get me through the night. This was what I called a dive bar.

Before I could order a drink, I was whisked away onto the dance floor by a very butch woman. I decided to just go with it and danced. When the song ended, I made my way to the bar where she followed and insisted on buying me a drink. I kept telling her I was fine and I will just have water.

Michelle stood back having a giggle at my expense. I motioned to her that she owed me for brining me here. When the woman left, I knocked back two tequilas and chatted to Michelle, then put money on the pool table to book a game of pool, which used to be one of my favourite pass times.

While we waited for our turn on the pool table, we had another few shooters and chatted to all the locals, enjoying ourselves. While we were playing pool, we heard motorbikes pulling up and the next thing about twenty guys walk in from the Crusaders Bike club.

I was all over this Sons of Anarchy here we come and asked one of the bikers that walked in wearing his cuts that I would like to know more about the club.

I don't know what possessed me, but I had no filter and asked him if he was gay purely because he was wearing an aftershave that my best friend who is gay wore all the time. He leant in and took my face in his big hands and planted a kiss on my lips. It was soft, wet and hard enough to get the message through that he was very straight. Then he walked away.

I had not been kissed like that in so many years and started to feel a tingle that I had not felt in a long time.

That night when we left I could still smell his aftershave on me. I smiled to myself and looked at Michelle then giggled and told her that I had the most fun in years.

I fell asleep and before long Michelle's phone rang. She shot up straight in the bed.

"Trace, wake up, the guys from the Crusaders are coming for coffee."

Although it was 4 am, we invited them to come for coffee.

I started to panic, and I told her I had no milk.

"No problem," I said, I called them and told them to bring milk.

In fifteen minutes, it sounded like thunder rolling into our road, loud enough to wake the dead, with six bikers on Harley's with a two-litre milk coming for coffee.

I don't know why I was afraid. Although I was a single woman, I was not yet divorced even though Percy had moved on, I still felt like this was wrong.

Michelle told me to 'live a little'. I felt like a naughty school girl staying up passed her bedtime but there was a rush that was familiar that came with it and it reminded me of the girl I used to be.

This watered-down version of me was not someone I liked very much. I had always been very spontaneous, but I guess that a failed marriage and a physical disability can make anyone shy away from things that once gave them that rush until you found your next one.

The bikers came for coffee. They were perfect gentlemen. I was surprised that these men were not drug dealers or arms dealers that one was an accountant and the others had regular jobs. It was an eventful early morning coffee with much laughing and then they left.

They said that if I ever 'needed anything they would gladly help'.

I never heard from them or contacted them again. I could feel that spark was alive in me once again, my inner rebel was out to play.

Now, I had been registered on the dating sites, I started to go on date after date, some were good, many were bad. On one date, I snuck out the back of a restaurant with the help of a waiter to get away from a man who was a not playing with a full deck of cards and I was not going to stay around to see what deck he had.

This guy started talking from the time I got there and when the waiter came to take our order he did not break sentence until he was asked again what would you like to order. The next thing, he flung his arm around me like he had known me all my life I was not comfortable and he just carried on talking. I'm pretty sure he never even noticed that I had left.

Dating sites are essentially the new way to meet people but I must admit, I miss the old conventional way, however I decided to embrace change.

As the dates got more frequent, I saw a pattern and started to analyse every profile that was on the sites and enjoyed the good dates.

When you understand the chemistry of love, what you experience going into a new relationship will help you understand the rollercoaster feelings so let me break it down.

The Chemistry of Love Explained

Love is very much a part of life and living on this planet. Love is about relationships, connection, mutual respect, honour, trust, pro-creation, family and yet when we are seeking love, most of us do not understand or know the basics of how we fall in love. When I think of 'The Chemistry of Love' it just makes sense, wish I had known this sooner.

There are three distinct stages lust, attraction and bonding, and they are mutually exclusive, which means they don't have any specific rules; some can occur, some might not.

These three distinct stages we can identify in terms of physiology as to what happens to our body when we fall in love.

Stage 1—Lust

Lust in its basic form is when the body floods with for the guys testosterone, for the women oestrogen and that releases that instinct and drive to procreate. It is essentially the desire to physically have intercourse, that is it!

Now, for guys there is a decrease in the bonding hormone oxytocin because of an increase in testosterone. For our ladies, oestrogen releases the little bit of our testosterone and oxytocin our bonding hormone.

I know, sometimes when they smell nice, look hot and tickle your grey matter, it can get hot under the collar so hence the 8 date rule, and this explains why in the initial stages of meeting, it's so important to get to know someone because some people will literally go for the lust.

Have you ever felt that 'hot under the collar feeling before'?

Stage 2—Attraction

Attraction is usually the stage when you start to build deeper bonds with a person. During this stage, our bodies increase dopamine release. Dopamine is the hormone related to pleasure, satisfaction and motivation. Our bodies are truly fascinating because anything that makes us feel good and increases the release of this feel good hormone becomes 'slightly addictive'. And that comes to us in this stage of attraction as that feeling of not being able to get enough of this person.

Something else to note while dopamine release is increased the hormone serotonin decreases. This is the hormone responsible for our moods, sleep. It is in this state that we can become obsessive and behaviour such as OCD arise and in a new relationship it shows up for example as: Why didn't they text? Why are they taking so long to reply to your text, obsessive behaviour in the relationship? While serotonin decreases in this attraction stage at the same time noradrenaline which is a stress hormone is released. So, here we are feeling attracted and feeling good but stressed at the same time. The attraction stage can be a roller coaster of emotions?

Stage 3—Bonding

The bonding stage happens over time it can be a few months even years for some people to get to this stage. Two chemicals are released in this phase and for woman it is oxytocin and for men it is vasopressin. Oxytocin for woman is known as the love hormone or cuddle hormone and vasopressin is known as the bonding hormone.

Stage three shares with us that bonding happens over time. Give yourself time to fall in love, hence my 8 date rule. That way you set yourself up for love match success.

> *"Love is a feeling you cannot explain tickles the heart and buggers your brain."*

My wall was up so as much as some of these men liked me and wanted more. I friend-zoned them faster than the Flash.

You have to kiss a lot of frogs to find your prince.

At one point, I found a connection with one suitor, we went on many dates and became involved without a label. We spent loads of time together, laughing and enjoying a whiskey or many. He stole many delicious kisses from me in his car when dropping me off.

I felt desired. Exhilarated. Enjoyed the rush from the chase.

He eventually asked me to come spend a night at his place. I was so nervous as I had not been intimate with anyone since Percy. I was going to be in someone else's arms. This excited me but I was over thinking it too much. The chemistry was insane.

176

That night, after talking under the stars and sipping on whiskey he said, "Let's go to bed."

I felt a little excited and anxious at the same time as I wheeled towards the bed. I had so many thoughts going through my head and my body was aching to be touched. Then I fell out of my wheelchair and landed on the floor.

He rushed into the room and asked me what happened.

My sense of humour kicked in.

"I fell for you!" I said.

We both laughed as he lifted me into bed. Something did not feel right, something deep inside me told me as much as I wanted it, I was not ready. Sadly, nothing happened except we spooned the whole night. I lay awake trying to make sense of what was going on with me.

The following morning, we spoke and decided to be friends. Today, I have the most amazing friendship with this man. I do believe that we were right for each other, but that timing was off. I needed more time to work on myself and to enjoy the freedom I fought so hard to regain.

New matches were coming through on the dating app. I was back on the market and enjoying the attention.

A new book was being born at this point and some insightful writing poured in.

I am no Gugu when it comes to love and relationships, just look at my two failed marriages, but I can tell you that we get into relationships for the wrong reasons. That is what my takeaway with this new book would be about. If we don't heal the hurt, we just bleed into the next relationship, which will be doomed to fail.

I met Andrew on Facebook, someone I had never met before. While scrolling, his profile popped up and I forwarded him a DM on Facebook messenger, saying something like "Hi, didn't know you were on the market!"

We shared a few conversations on WhatsApp, then Andrew invited me to lunch so we could meet face-to-face.

I got to the restaurant early and waited. I was just meeting a friend, no expectations and was not going to fall into another love trap. When Andrew arrived at the restaurant, I recognised him from Facebook and knew this was definitely not a Catfish.

He walked up to the table and greeted me. We immediately connected and started to talk, our conversation and banter was just what was needed and a little cheeky. We had wine and something to eat, then he excused himself to go have a cigarette, telling me that he was a social smoker, which did not bother me too much. Normally, a smoker for me was a deal breaker, but I had found a fellow sapiosexual person to talk to.

During our conversation, I asked him how he would know if his date wanted to be kissed? Andrew started to do a little dance for me which was rather sexy and was rather nice knowing other people in the restaurant could see him too. When he was done, he walked up to me and gave me a long wet passionate kiss.

I giggled when he pulled away and thought to myself: *Cheeky but nice.*

The rest of that afternoon, we sipped wine and exchanged stories. The lunch came to an end and all I could think was that I would really like to see Andrew again. I thoroughly enjoyed his company, and the chemistry was definitely there, but I wasn't sure what he thought about me.

The next time I saw Andrew, he came round to my house, and we sat on the couch talking and listening to music, sipping wine and lots of beautiful wet passionate kisses.

It felt so comfortable. I never once felt like I had a disability as he treated me exactly like any other woman, which was refreshing.

We met up quite a few times, then my home was sold, and I had to move, but I had a few days between moving that I needed somewhere to stay.

I tried to book a hotel for the weekend, so I had my own space before moving. I could not get a booking and told Andrew about all the hotels being fully booked due to polo championship. He told me he would have a look and when he called me to confirm that he had confirmed a booking, I asked how much it would cost and he refused to tell me. It made me feel uncomfortable as I was used to paying my way and this was very new to me.

That Friday afternoon, I booked into the hotel and Andrew called and asked if he could visit. He said he would bring wine and I agreed, I had packed snacks for the weekend, and I was ready for a chill time but that little voice inside me told me that Andrew's visit was going to be more than a visit. I did not want to think about it, so I put it out of my head.

When Andrew arrived, I noticed he had a bag with him.

'Oh crap! Is he staying over?' I questioned myself.

Panic stations sounded.

'Was I ready for this?'

Before long, we were sitting and enjoying each other's company and sipping wine, listening to music. Andrew leant in and kissed me. I could feel that he desired me, my body was on fire.

I craved what was to come, he took the glass from my hand put it on the nightstand and pulled me into the centre of the bed where he peeled off my clothes like unwrapping a present for the first time.

In years, I hadn't been touched like a woman and made love to with passion. I had forgotten what an amazing rush it was and the release that came, and it felt good.

Andrew had given me back something that had been missing for years. Being desired.

This was one of many sessions to come (pardon the pun). There were no labels attached. I was living in the moment and making up for lost time with Andrew.

When December arrived and my kids were out of town, I decided to go to Cape Town now that the divorce was through.

I stayed at a friend's to house-sit and spent Christmas and most days with my cousin. We had loads of fun, but when I was alone at the house, I was house sitting. I realised that I missed Andrew and my guard was down.

I started to question everything and felt vulnerable, which was not like me.

I spoke to Andrew over December and told him that I really missed him and wanted to see him, but I needed to get him out of my system.

When I was supposed to return to Johannesburg, I had caught COVID. I was gone a month and was not sure what Andrew was thinking as he was very secretive too.

When I arrived in Johannesburg, I did not see Andrew for a while and had mixed feelings about our situationship. I knew I was not ready for labels, but I just could not get enough of Andrew. I was insatiable when he was around and mostly because I felt desired by him, the way he would look at me even when we were just talking.

The chemistry between us was so magnetic that it scared me.

He came to see me one evening and was running a temperature. He had told me he had a COVID test, and it was negative but did not know why he was feeling so ghastly.

I never heard from him for a while and sent him messages which when unanswered. I started to panic not knowing what was going on, only to discover that he was on holiday in Zanzibar.

He was in ICU fighting for his life a hospital in Darah Salam, as he had contracted Malaria earlier before leaving South Africa. A WhatsApp came through from his son letting everyone know what had happened to Andrew.

Not once did he tell me he was going away. I felt a little disappointed that he would choose not to tell me.

'*Why was he being so secretive?*' This set off alarm bells and my wall came up, I was not going to get hurt again. I have trust issues and I just needed that one question mark to make me not trust him.

At this stage, I realised that I had developed feelings for Andrew, which was new for me. It was a major red flag. I did not need my heart crushed again and decided to move to Cape Town where there would be distance between us.

I had not told him as yet, because he had just come out of hospital after being flown back to South Africa.

When he finally came to see me, he was yellow with jaundice and still was not feeling himself. My heart still skipped a beat when I saw him. There was this magnetic chemistry between us.

I then mentioned by the way that I was moving to Cape Town. He was surprised as he wasn't sure what the boxes were for.

Soon, I left and moved to Cape Town. I thought this was the end of this unlabelled situationship but then I got a call from Andrew to say he was in Cape Town.

There I was, back in his arms, having every inch of my body pleasured.

I am still finishing my 30 dates to complete my book. The formula that I have put together is aimed at anyone looking for a meaningful relationship.

I have learnt from past relationships that a good strong connection is what needs to come first not the physical aspect.

Situationships never work because someone always catches feelings and that leads to heartache. I put an end to this undefined relationship. Andrew is a good man and I know we will remain friends going forward but for me, I know my worth and deserve a man that is emotionally available to share my life with.

Relationships don't need to be complicated, they just need honesty and communication but above all respect. I realised I would rather be alone than being someone's option. Half-backed relationships don't work for me. I rather like my company and know the right man will find his way into my life.

I do long for a meaningful committed relationship with someone who can match my energy and passion, someone who will be my best friend, my person and emotionally available.

I am a high value woman and know my worth now.

No one remembers how you start only how you finish!
Tracy Swinson

Chapter 13
Unbreakable

I sit here in the present writing this final chapter of my book but yet it is not the final chapter of my life. This has truly been a bumpy ride with highs and lows. I have been humbled by life experiences and I have grown as a human.

Within the cathedral walls of my heart, I can truly say that my faith has carried me through all these lessons.

One of my favourite lessons is 'Looking ridiculous for a moment is better than living your life with regret.'

Each lesson and experience has given me the skills to deal with whatever life throws at me and I have had a lot thrown at me.

Coming to Cape Town was the best decision I could have ever made. It was selfish but it was necessary, one would call it self-preservation. I needed the peace to collect myself and finish writing my book.

Not long after I arrived, I was introduced to Marlon who has become a close friend and creative cheerleader when it came to writing these chapters. He has pushed me when I was staring at blank pages.

My good friend Paula—remember her from my 2nd chapter—she is now a life coach and she called me up and offered me coaching sessions. I really needed it, I was feeling weathered and needed to put some perspective on my life.

The coaching came and went so fast but the tools that were given to me have been invaluable I feel you should be constantly up grading your life skills or taking on new hobbies.

Some of the tools I use on a daily basis which keeps me grounded is, asking myself "Is this the best decision for me?" "How does this make me feel?"

Then prioritising my day by honouring my yes and my no's. This means I have a list of to do's and when I find myself doing something not related, I ask myself. "Are you honouring your yes and no's?"

And I have realised the value of breathing exercises when you are stressed, it helps to relax you and refocus.

These tools are going to come into very good use going forward on my next journey.

Along with moving came something that was totally unexpected and this all happened last year 2022, one Sunday evening. I was sitting on the couch watching Netflix and felt my eyelids getting heavy so I decided to get off the couch and go to bed.

I went through my evening routine, brushing and flossing my teeth and facial routine, then went to pour myself some water to take to bed and I spilt some water as it fell, I felt it hit my foot.

I froze for a moment and thought, *Could this be?*

I leant forward and looked down at my bare feet, there was my left foot, covered in water.

I could feel the water fall onto my foot it felt wet and cold.

At this point, my heart was beating in my ears. Was I going mad? Had I spent too much time on my own and was I just imagining this? I went to my bedroom transferred onto the bed, pulling my legs onto the bed with them stretched out in front of me. I leant forward and touched my left foot it was indeed wet and cold.

There it was that 1%, I thought to myself as I pulled the covers up to my chin and snuggled down with a million thoughts of how and where do I go from here.

Is this going to be my final battle? Has everything else I went through set me up for this journey?

A few weeks went by. I said nothing. I was still grappling with what had happened. Then early hours of the morning, I woke up took a sip of water and stopped mid-sip. *Could it be I?* thought to myself. I could feel the duvet resting against my skin. This was crazy. I quickly sat up and when I pull the duvet off my legs I could feel it was no longer resting on my skin. I never went to sleep after that.

The next morning, when Marlon arrived I told him what had happened over the last couple of weeks. He suggested I should contact the Sports Science Institute in Cape Town this is where all the top South African athletes come to train or get treatment for injuries as well as ordinary people like me. I called and set up and appointment with the leading Biokinetics, Avanesh.

A few days later, Marlon and I got an uber to the appointment. I was so nervous wondering if I was setting myself up for disappointment. Was I going to hear what I heard all those years ago? *'Sorry, you will never walk.'* I quickly shut those thoughts out of my head and sat waiting for Avenesh to see me.

An athletic looking man called me into his office and opened a file. He started asking questions and taking notes. Nothing I said seem to faze him.

When he was done with the notes, he said, "Let's do a full neurological and physical assessment."

We went over to the plinth area where I transferred out of my chair and he started with the neurological assessment checking my body for sensation using a steel pointed object. I could not see where he was touching it on my body he would ask me if I could feel it and at what degree was the sensation.

He then moved onto the physical, putting me through my paces, checking my core strength and flexibility. He would put my legs in different positions then told me to move I tried my best but I could not but it felt like electrical pulses running up and down my legs.

When Avenesh was done he said, "Tracy, you have flickering muscle in your legs, feet and butt. I think, with the right program, you will be up on your feet again."

I started crying tears of joy there it was that 1% eighteen years later and I get the 1% to explore what I will get back.

Now, all that fighting and overcoming I did on my journey, to get to this today, was everything I needed to prepare me for the fight of my life the fight to stand and walk again.

And so, the training has begun and that will be to be continued in my next book. I can honestly say nothing I have gone through has been in vain, everything has prepared me for this next adventure in my life.

I stand humbled with gratitude, ready to take this challenge on.

PURPOSE—Today I sit writing the last chapter of this journey I have been on.

Looking back, I can't believe what I have actually endured. Tears of joy roll down my cheeks in disbelief that I have made it through this journey and truly like the woman sitting here today, the person I have become.

All the challenges, laughs, ups and downs have made me whom I am today.

I regret nothing. If I did, everything would have been in vain.

As I close this chapter on my life and look forward to the new one that awaits, I realise I was already a strong soul when I started out. All the hardships and explosion of emotions made me unstoppable. I believe we all have that strength if we learn to tap into it.

Every time you experience adversity in your life and come through it, there was a lesson attached to it and if you are smart enough to learn, you won't make the mistake again. I have learnt that we are not perfect, we will make mistakes, we will have hard times but it is how we face our challenges. You can have a 'can do' attitude or 'I can't' and that is the difference between making it or failing.

I have been to the dark side of brokenness where the abyss was suffocating and life was a huge question mark for me. Much like my mother did when she was ready to take her life and mine. But when given purpose, you push through and fight for your place in this world.

I wrestled with demons of my past that have haunted me for many years. Painful things I buried deep that surfaced when I started writing my book realising that most of my life I was fighting off the past and not dealing with the pain and loss I experienced.

In the pit of despair and wanting to give up, there had always been a little voice of hope deep inside me that encouraged me, nudged me forward. We all have that little voice inside us that guides and encourages us in good and bad times. Sometimes, our thoughts are so loud and we keep ourselves busy, so busy we can't hear this voice and life will even bring you to a standstill so you can be silenced long enough to touch the centre of your soul to connect with your inner voice.

This little voice inside me, my voice of reason, had been with me from the very beginning.

People look for the meaning in life and have done from the beginning of time. No-one has a definitive answer to the meaning of life or more personal what it means to you. I can say that for me it has been about the journey. My journey has been about finding strength when I thought I had none, finding hope when hope was lost and sharing my journey with others to inspire them to be overcomers too. There is no big mystery to life, just a journey we set off on and see how much we are able to grow along the way.

GRATITUDE—Feeling nostalgic, I looked through photos of myself and all the people in my life that have played a pivotal role.

My mum, Margret, who instilled in me the spirit of resilience; she also taught me the value of not ever giving up there will always be a reward at the end of each obstacle you face.

My three beautiful children: Kyle, Nicole and Greigan, without them I would never have experienced unconditional love, I would take a bullet for them any day, no questions asked.

My aunt Cynthia, who has been my pillar of strength and spiritual coach, edging me on using my faith to get through any situation leaning on the promises of God.

Everyone in my life, whether their intentions were good and bad, I feel nothing but gratitude. Each person and family member have impacted my life and taught me lessons without realising it. I say, thank you for these teachings and relationships.

Using the analogy of a piece of clay, it is what we all are when we are born. As time gathers momentum we are moulded by all the good and bad experiences. The amazing thing is that none of us are shaped the same. Then a day comes when the clay hardens and something in our life breaks this mould. We then have to gather the best pieces and put them together again with gold—this is a Japanese method of repairing cracks with gold—Kintsungi.

I guess what I am trying to say is that we are all beautifully broken and put together again just like Kintsungi.

CALLING—Through my hardships, I saw this as my purpose as it shaped and changed me into the person I am today, allowing me to follow what is now my calling: to share my story. Inspire others to keep their faith during hardships and have hope that they too will come through tough times.

INSPIRE—Today, I smile to myself as I glance over my shoulder and realise that the lessons and strength I carry forward are Tenacity, Humour, Resilience, Positivity, Gratitude and most of all UNBREAKABLE!

I close this chapter of my book knowing a new chapter in my life begins.

I heard a saying when I was a young girl, you know you lived a full life when you can write a book about it. Well, here you are. This is my journey and my book *Unbreakable*.

UNBREAKABLE

'Tis not the winter of discontent
Rather a deathly chill upon my breath,
I have faced life and now I face death.
Melancholy words of a life lay draped
Across my shoulders.
Death beckons and pauses
Then comes like a thief in the night
Death becomes me!
A new life is born from the abyss
Air has never smelt so sweet
Gratitude is how I feel
I see an explosion of all that can be
And so a new life, new chapter awaits
The peace I have now is worth what was lost
I emerge UNBREAKABLE!

Tracy Swinson

I know that each day holds the possibility of a miracle…it only takes 1%.
I am Unstoppable…perhaps two books!

Printed in Great Britain
by Amazon

36594136R00106